South Tyrol

**Studies in Austrian and Central European
History and Culture**

Günter Bischof, Series Editor

Austria in the Twentieth Century
Edited by Rolf Steininger, Günter Bischof,
and Michael Gehler

*South Tyrol:
A Minority Conflict of the Twentieth Century*
Rolf Steininger

Rolf Steininger

South Tyrol

A Minority Conflict of the Twentieth Century

Transaction Publishers
New Brunswick (U.S.A.) and London (U.K.)

Second printing 2009
Copyright © 2003 by Transaction Publishers, New Brunswick, New Jersey.

All rights reserved under International and Pan-American Copyright Conventions. No part of this book may be reproduced or transmitted in any form or by any means, electronic or mechanical, including photocopy, recording, or any information storage and retrieval system, without prior permission in writing from the publisher. All inquiries should be addressed to Transaction Publishers, Rutgers—The State University, 35 Berrue Circle, Piscataway, New Jersey 08854-8042. www.transactionpub.com

This book is printed on acid-free paper that meets the American National Standard for Permanence of Paper for Printed Library Materials.

Library of Congress Catalog Number: 2003047313
ISBN: 978-0-7658-0800-4
Printed in the United States of America

Library of Congress Cataloging-in-Publication Data

Steininger, Rolf, 1942-
South Tyrol: a minority conflict of the twentieth century / Rolf Steininger.
    p. cm.—(Studies in Austrian and central European history and culture)
Includes bibliographical references and index.
ISBN 0-7658-0800-5 (pbk.: alk. paper)
    1. Trentino-Alto Adige (Italy)—Politics and government—20th century.
2. Trentino-Alto Adige (Italy)—History—20th century. I. Title. II. Series.

DG975.T792S684   2003
945'.38091—dc21
                                                           2003047313

Table of Contents

Preface	i
Introduction	1
I. 1918-1922: From the Division of Tyrol to the March on Bozen	4
Partition and Annexation	4
24 April 1921: "Bloody Sunday" in Bozen	6
1 October 1922: The Fascists March on Bozen	10
II. Ettore Tolomei	14
III. 1922-1938: The Fascist Policy towards South Tyrol	21
The Name "Tyrol" Banned	21
Shutting Down the Press	25
Italianization of the Schools	26
Catacomb Schools	29
Additional Measures	32
The Fascist "Victory Monument"	35
The Destruction of Tyrolean Monuments	39
The Industrial Zone in Bozen	42
IV. 1939: Between Fascism and National Socialism — The Option	46
The Nazi *Völkischer Kampfring Südtirols* (VKS)	46
The Anschluß of Austria	48
The Hitler-Mussolini Agreement	49
The Position of the *Völkischer Kampfring Südtirols* (VKS)	55
To Go or to Stay? Disunity among the South Tyroleans	58
The Catholic Church	62

V. 1940-1945: Resettlement and "Reunification"	64
Resettlement	64
Nazi *Gauleiter* Franz Hofer	68
Resistance	74
The Founding of the South Tyrolean People's Party (SVP)	75
VI. 1945/46: South Tyrol and the Cold War	77
14 September 1945: No Return to Austria	77
In Rome and Vienna, the Battle Continues	82
Second Thoughts in Washington and London	85
VII. 1946: The Gruber-De Gasperi Agreement	97
VIII. 1948-1969: From Pseudo-Autonomy to the "Package"	112
"Break with Trient!"	112
Before the United Nations	117
The Bombings	122
The "Package"	129
IX. From the "Package" to the Present	136
Conclusion	145
Notes	150
The Gruber-De Gasperi Agreement	154
Chronology	156
Abbreviations	158
Further Literature	160
Acknowledgements	162
Index	164

Preface

Twenty years ago, I first taught a course on "The History of the Tyrol" to a dozen eager students of the University of New Orleans Summer School in Innsbruck, Austria. These young Americans became excited about a seemingly obscure subject such as regional Central European history. What were the themes of my course?

Historically speaking, whoever was in charge of Tyrol controlled the crucial Alpine passes that constitute a vital commercial and strategic crossroads of Europe. At a 4,000 feet elevation, the Brenner Pass is considerably lower than the principal Swiss Alpine transverses. The snow melted earlier in the spring on the Brenner, and traffic could be resumed weeks and months ahead of the Swiss passes. Roman generals and emperors crossed with their armies to preserve the *Pax Romana*. Medieval German Holy Roman emperors crossed regularly with their huge retinues to be crowned by the Pope in Rome. At the height of the Renaissance, the rich and fabled traders of Venice, Italy, and Augsburg, Germany, regularly crossed the Brenner with their precious wares. Art, architecture, ideas, and lifestyles filtered across these Alpine routes, too, and left some extraordinary legacies along the towns and villages of this vital crossroads over the main ridges of the Alps.

Politically, the principalities, counties, and bishoprics (ancient ones like Brixen!) were eventually unified by local nobility into the historic county of Tyrol in the High Middle Ages. When this local lineage died out in 1363, the Habsburg dynasty in Vienna acquired Tyrol. In the late fifteenth and early sixteenth centuries, Emperor Maximilian I, a principal builder of the Habsburg global empire, made Innsbruck his imperial capital off and on. The mineral riches of Tyrol elevated this region for a brief while to become a European hub. As the center of the European world shifted from the Mediterranean to the Atlantic, Innsbruck and Tyrol reverted back to the status of provincial Habsburg dominion. When the Western Allies defeated Austria-Hungary and the German Empire in World War I, the Habsburg Empire collapsed. President Woodrow Wilson's principle of "self-determination" cut the Habsburg dominion into pieces. A host of nation states emerged in Central and East Central Europe. Austria became a leftover, the "state that nobody wanted."

To gain a "strategic" border, Italy, one of the victor states, claimed the part of Tyrol south of the Brenner. The peacemakers in Paris met Rome's demands in 1919. This produced cheer in Italy and enormous incredulity and eventually hatred in the divided Tyrol and Austria. This historic land of Tyrol was one of the rare regions where President Wilson blatantly broke his promise for "self-determination." Tyrol had been a proud Habsburg province for almost 600 years. Now the Alpine ridge, which had united it for so long, cut it into two. The southern part became Italy's northernmost province, the northern and eastern parts ended up with Austria. This painful division was never tolerated by the North Tyroleans and even less by the roughly quarter million German speakers that were left with Italy. Families were left on both sides of the border. Herein lay the birth of one of twentieth century Europe's persistent and seemingly irresolvable minority conflicts.

No one is better qualified to tell this tale of sorrow and ultimate redemption than Professor Rolf Steininger. Historical discourse on the South Tyrol conflict has been laden with blatant nationalist historiography from both sides of this issue. Transplanted from northern Germany to Innsbruck, Steininger brings the necessary restraint not to be suckered into this nationalist/patriotic historiography. His emotional distance produces an analysis *sine ira et studio*. His small book tells the extraordinary tale of the ups and downs of this minority conflict through the violent blood-drenched history of European "ethnic cleansing" in the twentieth century. His is a tale of great power skullduggery versus resourceful local resistance. His is a story of old-fashioned diplomatic intrigue and backroom political skills and power plays. His is a cautionary tale about great power arrogance failing to wipe out gritty local survival instincts. Time would whittle down the stubborn resistance to compromise of the principal players. A skillfully constructed complex solution emerged which Steininger presents as a model solution for ethnic conflicts. In the end, reason prevailed.

In 1995, Austria joined the European Union (EU). Italy had been a founding member of the core group of nations that started the process of European integration. In this new Europe, such long-standing minority conflicts seem outdated. Historical conflicts are muted, and formerly hostile nationalities co-exist. Mutually acceptable historical narratives are constructed. In "Schengen-Europe," EU internal national boundaries such as the one between Italy and Austria along the Brenner are losing their importance. For all these reasons, Steininger's book deserves a larger readership beyond the local interested publics.

I wish this neat and compact book had been available to my students twenty years ago. Then I had a hard time finding any introductory texts in English for an interested American audience. Steininger's book will fill this gaping lacuna. It will also compliment the text *Austria in the Twentieth Century*, the first volume in our new CenterAustria series "Studies in Austrian and Central European History" which Dr. Steininger co-edited. One can only wish the drama of this story, which includes Hitler and Mussolini as principal actors, a wide readership.

Günter Bischof, New Orleans, November 2002

Introduction

South Tyrol, a region in the heart of the Alps about half the size of Connecticut, is a wonderful place with wonderful people. There is the saying that when this place of mountains and valleys was created, the Creator was in a particularly good mood.

The history of this place in the twentieth century, however, has not always been bright and beautiful. There was the First World War, with its devastating consequences and the "peace treaties" that only served to cause or exacerbate so many ethnic problems. Tyrol, a province that had been a part of Austria for over 500 years and was almost totally German-speaking, was split in two, and the southern part awarded to Italy as "spoils of war." The border drawn at the Brenner Pass cut South Tyrol off from an Austria then too weak to prevent the loss.

What followed, in a first phase, was the systematic subjection by the Italian Fascists of what had been a regional majority in South Tyrol, but was now a minority within Italy. In a second phase, Italians from the south with a totally different mentality swamped the country in order to get an Italian majority. Then, with the emergence of National Socialism in Germany, and eventually with the Hitler-Mussolini Agreement of 1939, there was a third phase: an experiment in "ethnic cleansing" called the "Option." As a result, 86 percent of all South Tyroleans agreed to leave South Tyrol and become citizens of "Greater Germany." Approximately 75,000 did actually leave. The effects of this decision can be traced from the highest levels of government down to the tiniest villages, and have not been forgotten to this day.

In the Second World War, Italy was first on one side and then on the other, with corresponding consequences for South Tyrol. The postwar period found an Italy purporting to be democratic and a South Tyrol caught up quite early in the machinations of the Cold War. The victorious powers rejected the return of South Tyrol to Austria and were steadfast in maintaining the Brenner border, although pressure from the British did result, in 1946, in an agreement between Italy and Austria on autonomy for South Tyrol. Germany no longer played a part in these years, so it was the Austrian Second Republic that would assume the role of "protector" of South Tyrol. Austria was then also occupied and weak, however, and would become actively involved only after the State Treaty of 1955, which finally restored to Austria its full independence.

In 1948, Italy granted South Tyrol an autonomy that proved to be none at all. By the late 1950s, disappointed hopes had aggravated the discontent and led to demands for real autonomy and even self-determination. Austria took the issue to the United Nations in 1960. When negotiations failed, there were bombings and later even fatalities. In 1963, a new center-left coalition government in Italy had more understanding for minorities and opened the way for constructive discussions. By 1969, negotiations had produced a plan for a new autonomy that came to be known as the "Package." It took two more decades to implement it. Finally, in 1992, Austria and Italy officially ended their dispute with an autonomy agreement for South Tyrol that could well serve as a model for approaching the problems that will accompany new nationalisms in the new century.

Today, the marks of this history are readily apparent. About forty kilometers south of the Olympic city of Innsbruck lies the Brenner border, beyond which the villages have both German and Italian names. To the surprise of German-speaking tourists, it is suddenly Italy, where Italian is spoken as well as German. To the surprise of tourists from Italy, German is spoken, as well as Italian. The central square of Bozen, the capital of South Tyrol, is Walther Square, named after the great medieval German poet Walther von der Vogelweide. His statue dominates the square, where one can sip an Italian cappuccino served by an Italian waiter and ponder how all this came about.

The two ethnic groups have lived in a state of mutual hostility for decades. On the South Tyrolean side, there has been justifiable mistrust. After all, the Italians have felt and acted as masters of a house that, from the South Tyrolean perspective, was not even their house. For the Italians, the South Tyroleans were *allogeni* (foreigners) or *valligiani dalle calze bianche* (flatlanders in white knee socks). Even after 1945, they did not understand the South Tyroleans — neither their customs and habits nor their language — and saw no reason to try to understand these *alloglotti* (speakers of a foreign tongue). After all, this was Italy! South Tyrol was now Italian territory and would remain so! Or maybe not? From this mixture of suspicion, ignorance, and arrogance inevitable conflicts have arisen, but in recent years the distrust has subsided somewhat. Today there is a formal, distanced cooperation, though by no means are the two groups living and working together in close cooperation. One reason for this has been that the Italians know little if anything about the history of this land. Indeed, this can be said of some German-speaking South Tyroleans as well, especially the young people, not to mention people in other countries.

Perhaps this work will encourage a better understanding of the history of South Tyrol. An Italian version entitled *Alto Adige/Sudtirolo 1918–1999* was published in 1999 simultaneously with the German original *Südtirol 1918–1999*. In the present volume, I have adapted the German version for the English-speaking reader, translating parts myself.

For a more detailed and comprehensive treatment of the topic "South Tyrol," see my works published by *StudienVerlag: Südtirol im 20. Jahrhundert. Vom Leben und Überleben einer Minderheit"*, Innsbruck-Vienna 1997, 1999 (quoted here as Steininger I), and *Südtirol im 20. Jahrhundert. Dokumente*, Innsbruck–Vienna 1999 (Steininger II), and for *1945/46 Los von Rom? Die Südtirolfrage 1945/46 und das Gruber-De Gasperi-Abkommen*, Haymon-Verlag, Innsbruck 1987 (Steininger III, with documents). Whoever would like to read more about the time from 1947 to 1969 might wish to consult my three-volume work (in German) *Südtirol zwischen Diplomatie und Terror 1947–1969* published by Verlagsanstalt Athesia, Bozen, under the auspices of the South Tyrolean Provincial Archive (Steininger IV). In addition, there a two articles in English: "Back to Austria? The Problem of South Tyrol in 1945/46" in *The European Studies Journal*, Vol. VII, No. 2, Fall 1990, pp. 51–83, and "75 Years After: The South Tyrol Conflict Resolved, A Contribution to European Stability and a Model for Solving Minority Conflicts" in *Contemporary Austrian Studies*, Vol. 3, 1995, pp. 189–206. For a thirty-page essay, documents, a detailed chronology (all in German) and further reading, visit the Institute of Contemporary History's online information service at <http://zis.uibk.ac.at/> Click first on "*SchwerpunktthemenI*" and then on "*Südtirol.*

If you are interested in South Tyrol today, click on <http://www.provinz.bz.it> to find lots of information in English and four other languages, as well as several links.

I. 1918-1922: From the Division of Tyrol to the March on Bozen

Partition and Annexation

The ceasefire between Austria-Hungary and Italy was signed on 3 November 1918 at the Villa Giusti in Abano in the vicinity of Padua. Up to this date, not one Italian soldier had ever stood on South Tyrolean soil. Only after the ceasfire began the uncontested occupation of South Tyrol by Italian troops, who had already reached Salurn, the Mendel Pass, and Schluderns by 4 November. Meran was occupied the following day. A cavalry patrol coming from the Mendel Pass reached Bozen on 6 November, and troops of the 7th Army finally occupied the city the next day. From Bozen, troops then proceeded through the Eisack Valley towards Brenner and occupied the Brenner Pass on 10 November.

A military government under General Guglielmo Pecori-Giraldi administered South Tyrol until 31 July 1919. Pecori-Giraldi had been born in 1856 in Florence, had taken part in the colonial wars in Eritrea (1903) and Libya (1911), and was named commander-in-chief of the Italian 1st Army in 1915. His job was to secure Italy's possession of South Tyrol, and the measures he carried out were consistent with this mission. First of all, on 18 November, came that famous bilingual proclamation posted in all South Tyrolean communities in which he laid out the fundamentals of his occupation policy.

The occupation of South Tyrol proceeded almost without a hitch; there were no serious incidents of which to speak. The population heeded the military's call to maintain order and discipline, and the soldiers comported themselves properly. It quickly became clear to the South Tyroleans that their land had been occupied and was under military administration. It was at once hermetically sealed off from Austria and all other foreign countries; thus all passenger and freight traffic with North Tyrol and Austria was halted. Telegraphic equipment and carrier pigeons had to be surrendered. Anyone failing to comply with these regulations faced a long prison sentence. The press was subject to strict censorship. Communication by mail and telegraph was also severely restricted. Letters could no longer be sent to Austria, Germany, Hungary, Bulgaria, and Turkey, and any letter coming from these countries was not delivered to the addressee. All other mail was subject to censorship.

Immediately following the occupation, the military high command in Padua, the *Comando Supremo*, forbade the importation of currency from Austria, although the Kronen in circulation were still considered legal tender. The German-speaking district officials were gradually replaced by Italian commissioners, which was certainly one of the military government's most draconian measures since a considerable portion of the Austrian administration was thereby eliminated. This was a clear violation of the ceasefire agreement, as was the decision simply to give government officials in South Tyrol the option of either applying to the Italian civil service for a job or resigning their posts.

Meanwhile, in Saint Germain near Paris, terms were not being negotiated, but dictated. In a petition to U.S.-President Woodrow Wilson, the mayors of all South Tyrolean cities and villages asked for help, but did so in vain. The peace conditions of 2 September 1919 constituted the end of the line for South Tyrol: cession to Italy without provisions for autonomy or minority protection. The Entente Powers disbursed the spoils of war they had promised in the London secret agreement of 26 April 1915 in return for Italy entering the war on their side.

On 6 September 1919, the National Assembly in Vienna agreed to the dictate by a vote of ninety-seven to twenty-three. Tyrolean representatives abstained as a sign of protest. For the South Tyrolean representatives, the time had come to take their leave. Eduard Reut-Nicolussi had the floor for his final speech, words that would become a legacy:

> In the face of this treaty, we say with every fiber of our being, with rage and pain: No! An eternal, irrevocable No! [Thunderous applause throughout the chamber, with spectators in the packed galleries joining in]... In South Tyrol, a desperate struggle will now begin for each farm, each townhouse, each vineyard. This will be a struggle utilizing all the weapons of the

mind and all the means of politics. And it will be a desperate struggle because we — a quarter of a million Germans — are being pitted against 40 million Italians in what is truly not a battle of equals.[1]

Four days later, Austrian Chancellor Karl Renner signed the Treaty of Saint Germain. A year thereafter on 10 October 1920, Italy passed the law that officially annexed South Tyrol, where this deed was referred to as an "abomination" before the eyes of history. A public appeal by the political parties characterized South Tyrol as a "victim of the peace treaty" and pointed to the denial of the right of self-determination. At the same time, the hope for "national liberation" was expressed. Nevertheless, the population was called upon "to abstain from any illegal activities, and to bear its fate with composure and dignity." There had been no incidents up to this point either.

24 April 1921: "Bloody Sunday" in Bozen

At this time, the Italian Fascists were just a nationwide gang of thugs who did not yet constitute a threat to the Italian state, although this would change very quickly. In Trentino and South Tyrol, all they were after initially was the removal of old Austrian symbols. Refusal by the local authorities to submit to their demands was labeled a "defilement of the nation" and answered with violence. Thus, on 12 February 1921, a truck convoy of Trentino Fascists drove to Auer and Salurn to remove all the "double eagles" they could find. A few days later, they tore down the German-language sign referring to "Bozen" (instead of Bolzano) at the headquarters of the civilian commissioner there. On 16 February 1921, Achille Starace, a lumber dealer originally from Apulia who was the leader of the Fascists in Trient, founded the *Fasci di Combattimento* of Bozen, a Fascist organization with 120 members, most of whom were businessmen from other parts of Italy or military officers. At the end of April, Luigi Barbesino, a lumber dealer originally from Piemont, took over leadership of the group, most of the supporters of which were railroad workers who had relocated there from other parts of Italy. Although the majority of them had been Socialists and Communists before coming to South Tyrol, they joined the *Fascio* soon after their

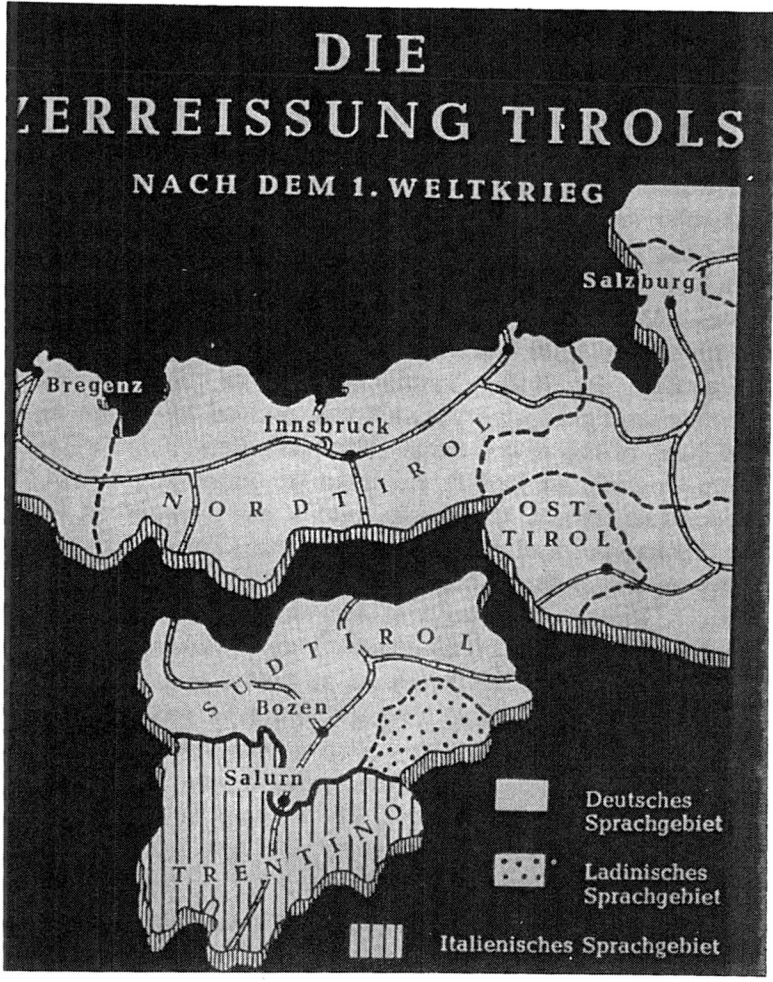

The Partition of Tyrol after World War I

The map shows the area where German, Ladin, and Italian are spoken and the new Austrian-Italian border following the Treaty of Saint Germain in 1919. The victorious powers do not draw the new border along the linguistic boundary south of Salurn, but rather arbitrarily at the Brenner Pass, which creates a long-term problem.

Source: Provincial Bureau for South Tyrol set up in 1945 by the government of the Province of Tyrol, Innsbruck, Austria.

arrival because the group was the leading exponent of the interests of ethnic Italian immigrants.

The first great outburst of Fascist violence was the assault on a *Trachtenumzug* (ceremonial procession of ethnic Germans wearing their traditional national costumes) on the occasion of the opening of the Bozen Fair on 24 April 1921. This event was infused with particular significance by the fact that, on the very same day, a plebiscite was taking place in North Tyrol on the Anschluß of the Province of Tyrol to the German Reich (98.5 percent voted for the Anschluß). Although the date for the Bozen Fair had already been set in November 1920, the Fascists suspected a connection with the referendum in North Tyrol. Furthermore, they regarded the *Trachtenumzug* as a provocation and decided to disrupt the event. The head of the new General Commission for Venezia Tridentina, Luigi Credaro, advised Rome about the impending events, but he received no answer. Meanwhile, the German Association, formed by the German political parties, requested that Credaro take appropriate steps to ensure their security. Moreover, the prefects of Mantua, Brescia, Vicenza, Verona, and Mezzolombardo informed Credaro a day before the event that the Fascist groups headquartered there were planning to go by train to Bozen to hold a counterdemonstration. Credaro took no precautionary steps; rather, he publicly declared that all possible measures to ensure security would be taken, but nothing at all was done. Thus the inevitable came to pass.

On the morning of 24 April, 280 Fascists from other regions of Italy arrived by train in Bozen, where they joined up with 120 members of the Bozen *Fascio*. All of them were properly equipped for the occasion. At the *Trachtenumzug*, they indiscriminately attacked participants and onlookers alike, swinging clubs, firing pistols, and throwing hand grenades. Franz Innerhofer, a teacher from Marling, was shot by a Fascist as he tried to protect two children. About fifty people were injured, all of them South Tyroleans. It was only after the attack that the military intervened, though not to safeguard the victims, but rather to protect the Fascists. They were escorted back to the train station, where they could embark on their return trip without hindrance. The Fascists seized the plebiscite ballot boxes in the Fair Center — set out to enable attendees to take part in the North Tyrol vote — and brought them to Trient where they were publicly burned.

The South Tyrolean population was stunned by what had taken place in Bozen, which had been totally unexpected. But Benito Mussolini made things crystal clear:

> If the Germans on both sides of the Brenner don't toe the line, then the Fascists will teach them a thing or two about obedience. South Tyrol is Italian and bilingual, and no one would even dream of trying forcibly to Italianize these German immigrants. But neither may Germans imagine that they might push Italy back to Salorno and from there to the Lago di Garda. Perhaps the Germans believe that all Italians are like Credaro. If they do, they're sorely mistaken. In Italy, there are hundreds of thousands of Fascists who would rather lay waste to South Tyrol than to permit the tricolore that flies above the Vetta d'Italia to be lowered. If the Germans have to be beaten and stomped to bring them to reason, then so be it, we're ready. A lot of Italians have been trained in this business.[2]

In North Tyrol, this incident was condemned in the strongest possible terms. For months, Tyrolean newspapers continually reported on "Bloody Sunday" and its consequences. As early as 28 April, the Andreas Hofer Association had organized a protest rally. Ten years later on 24 April 1931, a plaque was unveiled in Innsbruck commemorating the tenth anniversary of Innerhofer's death.

No one was ever brought to justice for Innerhofer's murder, although Prime Minister Giovanni Giolitti had called upon Credaro to immediately arrest and punish the perpetrators. The words were not followed up by deeds. In fact, two Bozen Fascists, Attilio Crupi and Vittorio Moggio, were held for a short time, but were then set free after Mussolini threatened to come to Bozen on 1 May together with 2,000 Fascists to force their release. The investigations by the *carabinieri* from Bozen and Verona went nowhere, probably because the police were unable to penetrate the well-organized Fascist groups. Shortly thereafter, pre-fascist Italy enacted one of the most far-reaching measures effecting South Tyrol: the "Lex Corbino" named after then-Minister of Education Mario Corbino. This was a special school law for the new provinces that required Italian parents to send their children to Italian schools. In implementing this legislation, Credaro's primary objective was "to establish firmly and strengthen the numerical, political and cultural position of the Italians in South Tyrolean schools."

What appeared to be a measure to protect the Italian minority became, in its implementation, an "offensive weapon" aimed at South Tyrol. Strictly monolingual Italian commissions that went about their business in ruthless fashion ascertained families' ethnicity. They made the effort to ascribe Italian nationality to as many families as possible in order to oblige them to sent their children to Italian schools. In doing so, they simply declared families with Italian or Italian-sounding names to be Italian, even if they spoke German; such was also the case with family names that ended with "a" or "o." The Ladins (who spoke a Rhaeto-Romanic language) were likewise made into Italians, and their children forced to attend an Italian school. The impact was particularly hard in the South Tyrolean Unterland, where forty-nine German elementary schools were closed and the German pupils forced to attend Italian schools. Criminal charges were filed against parents who refused to comply; protesting to Rome was pointless.

1 October 1922: The Fascists March on Bozen

On 18 March 1922, Luigi Facta became prime minister. He was even weaker and less of an authority figure than his predecessor Ivanoe Bonomi, and the end of his administration was marked by the victory of the Fascists with their notorious March on Rome. This concluded an eight-month domestic political crisis during which South Tyrol had been shifted onto Italy's back burner. The focus was on the future of the state, not on the interests of some tiny minority. By the late summer of 1922, the Fascists controlled all of Italy with the exception of parts of the south, Sardinia, and South Tyrol. At the end of October came their March on Rome with which they took power over the entire state. The "dress rehearsal" for this march was conducted in South Tyrol. On 6 April in Trient, the Fascists of Venezia Tridentina decided on a plan of action for South Tyrol featuring the following demands:

- the introduction of Italian law as quickly as possible;

- the elimination of any sort of autonomy in lawmaking and administration;
- a single province encompassing the whole of Venezia Tridentina;
- the dissolution of the civilian general commission, the central bureau for the new provinces, and the regional and central administrative bodies;
- the use of the Italian language in all public offices (though maintaining the right of the South Tyroleans to conduct official business in German);
- the inclusion of Italian as a required subject in all German-language schools;
- military training for young South Tyroleans males in other Italian provinces; and
- the disbandment of political and political-athletic associations that pursued irredentist aims.

Three weeks later, they followed up these words with deeds. On 27 April, they demanded that the City of Meran use both German and Italian in all official notices and announcements of the spa administration as well as in the designation of streets, and that a church be made available to the Italians to hold their religious services. At the same time, the "flag dispute" began with the Fascist demand that the Italian *tricolore* be flown from City Hall. The local Fascist Party organization that had formed in Meran in the meantime had raised the Italian flag that has always been a symbol of *Italianità* above Tyrol Castle. (There had been a similar incident involving a flag in Salurn shortly before. The German-speaking local priest, Simon Delueg, refused to consecrate an Italian flag that was for him the banner of a "government of Freemasons headed by a king whom the Pope had excommunicated.") When the Meran City Council refused to give in, the Fascists reiterated their demands in the form of an ultimatum and threatened to resort to violence if the City Council failed to comply. On 24 August, it abandoned further resistance.

Mussolini characterized the methods employed in Meran as an example to be followed throughout South Tyrol. In his opinion, a similar ultimatum ought to be used to break the resistance in Bozen, which is exactly what happened in early October. The Fascists under Francesco Giunto and Alberto de Stéfani occupied a school, the *Elisabethschule*, which was renamed Scuola Regina Elena at a Fascist ceremony on 2 October. That afternoon, 700 Fascists occupied the City Hall, which was being guarded by 180 *carabinieri* and soldiers. Although the government had ordered that the building be defended, it fell to the Fascists without a fight. In a telegram to Prime Minister Facta, they described themselves "as the interpreters of the nation's feelings" and demanded that the government protect the Italianness of this land that was being subjected to such humiliation and repression. They called for the dismissal of the responsible politicians and their replacement by those who would make possible an effective exercise of Italian sovereignty. In their view, provincial and communal autonomy was no longer justified and should be revoked at once. De Stéfani, who later became Minister of Finance under Mussolini, personally wrote to Facta:

> No less than four years after liberation, Fascist action makes it possible for a portrait of the King of Italy to be hung in Bozen City Hall. It is the duty of this government to see to it that those responsible are called to account, and to ensure that king and country are respected. Otherwise, all of Italy, from the Alps to the sea, will rise up against you.[3]

The occupation of City Hall lasted a few hours. Giunta and De Stèfani demanded the appointment of a commissioner to administer Bozen and the disbandment of the City Council, and the Italian authorities capitulated to the Fascists in this instance as well. Credaro dissolved the Bozen City Council, dismissed Bozen's long-time mayor Julius Perathoner, and named Augusto Guerriero commissioner. Guerriero was thus the first government-appointed mayor of Bozen. Immediately after taking office, he ordered that the *Elisabethschule* that had been occupied by the Fascists be operated as an Italian school in the future.

The dress rehearsal for the March on Rome had been a success. Mussolini commented on the march on Bozen in a speech delivered on 4 October:

Now we come to Bolzano. Here, we are on Italian soil where Italian law has jurisdiction. Who has safeguarded this? Fascism! Who has enforced the Italianness of a city that must be Italian? Fascism! Who drove out that man Perathoner who kept five Italian governments in check four years long? Who gave the Italians a school and a church, and who gave the Italians of Alto Adige a feeling of dignity? Fascism! Who displayed the bust of the king in the Bolzano City Hall? When the king himself was in Bolzano, he forgot to do it. Fascism! The Germans were astonished at the physically beautiful and morally superior Fascist youth. Those Germans who are living illegally on Italian territory, ask: "What kind of Italy is that?" We answer, "It is an Italy of quality, power and energy, that says: 'At the Brenner we are, and there we'll stay!' We do not desire to go to Innsbruck, but neither should you think that Germany and Austria will ever be able to return to Bolzano!"[4]

In *Popolo d'Italia*, he wrote, "The method that one must employ with Germans is the method of violence. . . . The war brought our political borders to the Brenner; now, Fascism brings you Italy!" What that meant for the future was made clear by the fascist South Tyrolean newspaper *Piccolo Posto* right after the action in Bozen:

A big job awaits us, one that must be done with tremendous energy. Germanism has to be eradicated from the soul just as its physical manifestations have been obliterated. This region must become Italian, and its inhabitants must become Italians, so that everything here is Italian and brings to mind only Italy.[5]

The groundwork for this policy had already been laid by one man: Ettore Tolomei.

II. Ettore Tolomei[6]

Ettore Tolomei was the most extreme Italian nationalist. One legacy of his doings is still evident in South Tyrolean communities to this day: the bilingual names of towns, villages, rivers, and the like. Taking possession of South Tyrol once and for all and Italianizing it were Tolomei's two most important concerns, and he made their realization — using practically any and all means possible — his life's work. Who was this man? Tolomei (1865-1952) grew up in a nationalistically oriented Italian family in Rovereto. In his early youth, his mother brought him into contact with South Tyrol, where he spent a great deal of time with his grandparents in Glen bei Neumarkt. In similar fashion, he became acquainted with the Dolomite Mountains in the vicinity of Cortina d'Ampezzo where relatives owned a hotel. After attending prep school in Rovereto, he entered college in 1883 in Florence, studying history and geography. He spent his sophomore year in Rome, where he became associated with the nationalistic Dante Alighieri Society. After graduation, he worked as a teacher, first in Tunis (1888), then in Italian schools in Salonika (beginning in 1894), Smyrna (1897) and Cairo (from 1898). In 1901, he returned to Italy and took a position in the Foreign Ministry's Office of the Inspector General of Italian Schools Abroad. His struggle for Italy's acquisition of South Tyrol had already begun in March 1890 with the appearance of the first issue of *La Nazione Italiana*, a weekly magazine he founded and co-edited. The self-appointed mission of this stridently propagandistic publication was the popularization of the nationalistic positions and cultural concepts of the Dante Alighieri Society. Furthermore, it was designed to contribute to promoting the group's irredentist ideas in the sense of emerging nationalism. The publication was clearly conceived as a work of vociferous advocacy and propaganda. Thematically, it dedicated the most space to essays on the two "classic objectives" of irredentism, Trient and Trieste, though numerous articles also treated other areas in the Levant and North Africa, and thus anticipated issues that would later comprise the platform of Fascist nationalism:

the dream of a Mediterranean empire and restoration of the grandeur of Ancient Rome.

Tolomei enthusiastically adopted the "natural boundary theory" that was being propagated at the time. He reported on this subject in the very first issue of *La Nazione Italiana*, underscoring his elaborations with cartographic illustrations. For him, the Ladinic element was of particular interest in *Alto Trentino*, as he then referred to South Tyrol. Indeed, at this time, he still acknowledged the ethnic uniqueness of the Ladins, but he considered the assimilation of their language into Italian to be a necessary precondition for the realization of his program. He regarded the Ladins and their culture as the Latin element in South Tyrol. Through the Italianization of the Ladins, he hoped to drive an Italian-Ladinic wedge into that German-speaking region that would then further "re-Italianization." The German-speakers were "intruders" into an Italian region, and these persons now had to face absorption or relocation.

In December 1890, *La Nazione Italiana* had to cease publication for financial reasons. Nevertheless, numerous elements of both form and content flowed out of Tolomei's first journalistic undertaking and into a later, larger-scale work, the *Archivio per l'Alto Adige*. The broad thematic spectrum of both publications — later, in the *Archivio*, limited to South Tyrol — encompassed a wide variety of articles dealing with history, geography, literature, art history, toponymy, economics, and folkloric studies. Furthermore, one can identify in the *La Nazione Italiana* that mode of argumentation that was characteristic of Tolomei, whereby ideological patterns of thinking exert a determinative influence on articles written with a claim to scholarly authoritativeness.

Tolomei worked as a journalist for the magazines *Giornaletto* and *Minerva* before founding the *Archivio per l'Alto Adige*. In 1904, he also climbed the Glockenkarkopf (also known as Glockenkarkofel) in the Ahrntal Alps – declaring his effort a first ascent, although Fritz Kögel had already accomplished that feat in 1895. Tolomei dubbed the peak "Vetta d'Italia," a choice of names consistent with the "natural boundary theory" and endowing the region with the superficial appearance of Italianness. In doing so, Tolomei made a bold statement in support of his struggle to gain South Tyrol for

Italy. The instrument in this struggle would be the *Archivio*, which premiered in August 1906 in Glen bei Neumarkt.

In accordance with the program of the *Archivio*, which claimed scientific authority and strict objectivity — although the discrepancy between pretension and actuality was tremendous — Tolomei wanted to prove and propagate the "Italianness" of South Tyrol, and this claim to scientific authority seemed to be ensured by the contributions it ran by prominent scholars from throughout the Kingdom of Italy.

Tolomei himself maintained that the first issue of the *Archivio* — both as a work of journalism and as the manifestation of an idea — had to be tantamount to treasonous screed for the Austrian-Tyrolean public. He even reported with pride on German demonstrations against him and the *Archivio* in Neumarkt.

But this was only one facet of Tolomei's activities. He also put out flyers giving information on "true" ethnographic conditions in South Tyrol, and distributed postcards with cartographic depictions of the region. The account of his ascent of the Vetta d'Italia and lists of Italianized names of South Tyrolean villages were sent free of charge to *Archivio* subscribers. Magazine staffers were sent to cover all sorts of conferences put on by the Dante Alighieri Society and to the *Congressi geografici italiani*. Tolomei's undertaking prospered. The magazine soon enjoyed a large readership in Italy, and the Italian place names he had come up with gradually found their way into maps, textbooks, public transportation timetables, newspapers, and magazines. The fact that the quarterly journal's circulation included, above all, public and scholarly libraries indirectly enabled it to attain a high degree of authoritativeness, and, over time, it even assumed the character of a reference work or an original source. For the Italian population, it was, from 1914 on, the sole source of information on the South Tyrolean question.

Up to the outbreak of World War I, Tolomei succeeded in imparting the appearance of Italianness to the region between the Salurner Klause and Brenner, which the majority of his readers who were unfamiliar with local conditions interpreted as a generally binding legal entitlement. Indeed, the *Archivio* treated a wide variety of topics, though certain focal points gradually began to emerge; aside from contributions to illustrate natural boundaries, such as those associated with the watershed theory, toponymy assumed increasing importance. Tolomei conceived of these toponymic studies as the "re-Italianization" of the names of villages, geographical features, and even families that had been forcibly Germanicized purportedly not too long before.

Beginning in 1915, the *Archivio* was printed in Rome. In the "*Serie di guerra*" that began to run at this time, one notices a significant change in the publication's spectrum of topics as well as the makeup of its staff. From this point on, most of the articles were authored by Tolomei himself. The claim to scholarly authoritativeness of the *Archivio*, which was to have been ensured by collaboration with competent experts, now proved to be mere window dressing that, particularly during the war years, was only capable of thinly disguising the magazine's propagandistic tendencies. As early as 1915, Tolomei began disseminating detailed and comprehensive concepts of a possible annexation of South Tyrol and ideas about the steps that ought to be taken in this case. Several memoranda were sent to the prime minister at the time, to other important government officials, and to various nationalistic associations. As for the German population, it was anticipated that they would assimilate, although thoughts of a possible resettlement had already begun to surface. In Volume 11 of *Archivio* dated 1916, Tolomei published his first "*Prontuario dei nomi locali dell' Alto Adige*" with translations of approximately 10,000 village and place names. These were totally superficial translations, often displaying not even the slightest idea about the etymological significance of the German name; in some instances, an Italian ending was merely appended to a German designation. In the uncompromising way he went about this, Tolomei was unsurpassed. One effect of this was that, for the first time, the entirety of the indigenous nomenclature of place names, including the names of geographical features and farmsteads, were transformed into another language through one man's act of will.

Only a few Italian names were already in common usage: Bolzano for Bozen, Vipiteno for Sterzing, Egna for Neumarkt. In other cases, Tolomei took Roman or Late Latin names for which there was documentary evidence as his point of departure and simply Italianized them (for example, Appiano, derived from Castrum Appianum, for Eppan; Gschlier became Casteliere; Geschwell, Casabella). There were also instances in which he simply took

German place names and literally translated them into Italian (for example, Mezzaselva for Mittewald). Names containing *Dorf, Schloss, Knott, Schneide, Berg, Kopf* and so forth were no longer permitted in the Venetic valleys at the upper reaches of the Etsch. Many names are the result of simple phonetic changes to the German name to make them easier to pronounce, or even pure for example, Colle Isarco for Gossensass, because the church was situated on a hill (*Colle*) on the banks of the Eisack (Isarco) River.

An additional field of activity during the 1916-17 period was the preparation of maps for the *Istituto De Agostini*, which was set up to support Tolomei's efforts to bestow Italian names. These maps were used by the Italian delegation at the Paris Peace Conference, giving the impression that this was an old Italian region.

For Tolomei, the occupation of South Tyrol by Italian troops after the ceasefire of 3 November 1918 was a decisive step on the path to "retaking" South Tyrol. At this point, his chief objective was to radically alter the situation and to make it clear to the South Tyroleans that their land was in the possession of Italy once and for all, though this effort had only modest success. It was not until the victory of the Fascists that his big moment arrived. On 3 March 1923, he was appointed senator, and his influence on South Tyrolean policymaking grew steadily. An Italian newspaper wrote in April 1923: "He created Alto Adige. He created it in its current geographical conception; he forced it upon the historical consciousness of the nation through thirty years of work in that field." On 19 March 1923, Tolomei and Giovanni Preziosi, who would go on to be one of the most rabid anti-Semites, were officially assigned by Giacomo Acerbo, a leading Fascist, to put together a catalogue of measures for the Italianization of South Tyrol. Two days later, another meeting took place between Tolomei and Minister of Education Giovanni Gentile. On 29 March, King Victor Emanuel III signed the decree ordering the Italianization of village names on the basis of Tolomei's first *Prontuario*. The names of 300 villages were to be changed in this first phase. By 14 April, Tolomei's catalog was almost complete, and Minister of Finance De Stèfani announced that he was prepared to make available all financial means necessary to carry out the project. On 25 May, the measures were submitted to the Council of Ministers, and they were passed on 1 July as the "*relazione Tolomei-Preziosi*."

Tolomei's big moment in the spotlight came on 15 July 1923. In the Bozen Municipal Theater, which had been leased out to an Italian association a month before, Tolomei, accompanied by the thunderous ovation of an audience that had traveled to attend this event via specially chartered trains from Trient, announced his famous 32 "*provvedimenti per l'Alto Adige*," which the next day's edition of *Der Tiroler* characterized as "measures for the eradication of German culture in South Tyrol." Tolomei called for:

1. the unification of Alto Adige and Trentino to form a single province with Trient as its capital,
2. the appointment of Italian communal secretaries,
3. revision of the (citizenship) options and closure of the Brenner border to all persons to whom Italian citizenship had not been conferred,
4. provisions to make it more difficult for Germans and Austrians to get entry visas and permission for temporary residence,
5. provisions to prevent immigration by Germans,
6. revision of the 1921 census,
7. mandating Italian as the language of official government business,
8. the dismissal of German bureaucrats or their transfer to other provinces,
9. disbanding the German Association,
10. disbanding all mountaineering clubs that were not affiliated with the Italian Alpine Association and transfer of their mountain huts to the Italian Alpine Association,
11. banning the name "South Tyrol" and "German South Tyrol,"
12. shutting down *Der Tiroler*, the daily newspaper published in Bozen,
13. Italianization of German place names,
14. Italianization of public signs and inscriptions,
15. Italianization of street signs,
16. Italianization of German family names,
17. Removal of the monument to Walther von der Vogelweide from Walther Square in Bozen,
18. increasing carabinieri strength while also eliminating German units,

19. measures to facilitate the purchase of land and immigration by Italians,
20. measures to encourage foreign countries to maintain a policy of non-involvement in South Tyrol,
21. elimination of German banks and establishment of an Italian mortgage bank,
22. construction of customs offices in Sterzing and Toblach,
23. generous subsidies for the Italian language and culture,
24. construction of Italian kindergartens and elementary schools,
25. construction of Italian intermediate schools,
26. thorough investigation of university degrees earned abroad,
27. expansion of the *Istituto di Storia per l'Alto Adige*,
28. revision of the geographical dimensions of the Bishopric of Brixen and strict surveillance of the activities of the clergy,
29. use of Italian in civil and criminal court proceedings,
30. state control of the Bolzano Chamber of Commerce and the agricultural associations (corporazioni),
31. an extensive railroad infrastructure construction program in order to facilitate the Italianization of Alto Adige (Milan-Mals, Veltlin-Brenner, Agordo-Brixen rail projects), and
32. increasing troop strength in Alto Adige.

The program announced by Tolomei was carried out step by step over the following years, in which there were tactical variations and delays but nothing to change the overall strategy. Implementation can be divided into two phases: the time up through 1926, and then the period from 1927 on, during which Bozen was a separate province. In a second period, measures became more stringent and the life of the South Tyroleans became even more unbearable.

When the Fascists realized that it was obviously impossible to turn stubborn South Tyroleans into "good" Italians, they introduced a new element, called "majorification," that is, the destruction of ethnic identity through massive immigration of Italians, particularly from the south. Thus, the climate became more and more "inhospitable" to the South Tyroleans. Then, at the end of this process in 1939, there came the "Option," a kind of "ethnic cleansing," as we would call it today, the "final solution" to the South Tyrolean question through a more or less forced expulsion of the South Tyroleans.

III. 1922-1938: The Fascist Policy towards South Tyrol

The measures of the Fascist program under Mussolini had an impact on every aspect of South Tyrolean society. Let's examine these step by step.

The Name "Tyrol" Banned

By April 1923, Italian place names had already been introduced in South Tyrol in accordance with the directory that Tolomei had published in 1916. On 8 August, Prefect Giuseppe Guadagnini decreed that the use of the name "Tyrol" would be prohibited beginning on 23 August. All derivatives from and compounds including this word, such as "Tyrolean," "South Tyrolean," and "German South Tyrolean" were likewise banned. A few of the real hard-liners even demanded that the names of products like "Tyrolean loden" be changed. Violators were subject to imprisonment for up to a month or a fine of twenty to 200 Lira (increased in 1931 to 2,000 Lira — about three months' wages — and three months imprisonment). The newspaper *Der Tiroler* had to be renamed *Der Landsmann*; even the *Tirolia* publishing house received a new name: *Vogelweider*, which was later changed to *Athesia* (Latin for the river Etsch which flows through South Tyrol). The region from the Brenner to Salurn was now officially known as Alto Adige. In German, the terms "Oberetsch" and "Etschlaender" could be used for Alto Adige and Atesino. (In the first Autonomy Statute of 1948, this then became the *Tiroler Etschland* in German. The official reinstatement of the province's name — Südtirol — in the new Autonomy Statute of 1972 was then a belated act of historical justice.) In the last issue of *Der Tiroler* before the ban went into effect, the following appeared:

> Farewell, my land Tyrol! Now commences a new beginning; at the end, those who are not especially well disposed to us expect

us to be displaced as a people and uprooted from our homeland. We know what is in store for us. We are aware and we are maintaining our composure. But, before the government, the Italian people and the entire world, we will arise and relentlessly demand to know: What have we done to deserve this?

The South Tyrolean representatives in the Chamber of Deputies in Rome protested; an appeal to the public ended with these words:

Though the land is torn asunder, though South Tyrol has been absorbed by the Kingdom of Italy and become a part of the Province of Trient, our homeland is still, despite all the new names, that which it has always been, and the people will forever be what their fathers were: Tyroleans. We remain what we are; Tyrol will not disappear until its mountains are no more.

There were loud protests in North Tyrol too. The *Innsbrucker Nachrichten* wrote:

If those who rule the Tyrolean south believe that they can completely eradicate the name of our land by the stroke of a pen, then their power may perhaps succeed in obliterating the letters in writing and in print, but this will merely burn the name Tyrol that much hotter and deeper into the hearts of the Tyroleans. . . . We Tyroleans on this side of the Brenner have been just as deeply wounded by this dastardly deed on the part of Mussolini as our brothers in South Tyrol, and neither will we ever forget the name Tyrol . . . until one day, the wheel of history turns against those who have committed this outrage.

The *Tiroler Anzeiger* assured its readers that the name Tyrol would still be shining "long after Mussolini's star has set." The Innsbruck City Council then made an unmistakable gesture: It was decided to rename several streets and squares in Innsbruck and to give them the names of South Tyrolean cities. Thus *Bahnhofsplatz* became *Südtiroler Platz*, *Margarethenplatz* became *Bozner Platz*, *Rudolfstrasse* became *Brixner Strasse*, *Landhausstrasse* became *Meraner Strasse*, *Kaiser Wilhelmstrasse* became *Salurner Strasse*,

Bahnhofstrasse became *Brunecker Strasse* and, finally, *Südbahnstrasse* became *Sterzinger Strasse*. Mayor Wilhelm Greil called this act "a pledge of loyalty to South Tyrol" and stated, "Innsbruck wants to keep the world's conscience aware in its streets and squares," which it then succeeded in doing for a few years. (Nowadays, hardly anyone can recall this renaming.) In 1925, a South Tyrolean named Adolf Innerkofler described the situation as follows:

> The name Tyrol or South Tyrol could no longer be published in a newspaper or appear in any printed matter whatsoever. *Carabinieri* personally went through stores, taverns, and print shops, crossing out Tyrol or South Tyrol, even on picture postcards that had been printed long before, until the words were completely illegible. You were not even allowed to say "Tyrolean dumpling"; you had to say "Oberetsch dumpling."[7]

No sooner had the name "Tyrol" been banned than the authorities launched their offensive against organized clubs and associations. On 3 September 1923, the South Tyrolean Alpine Association and all its local affiliates were dissolved; in early 1924, all of their assets, including seventy-seven mountain huts, were turned over to the Club Alpino Italiano.

If one's aim is to cause a minority to lose its national identity, then one must first deprive it of its language. This the Fascists did in purposeful fashion. Ever since 30 November 1922, correspondence with the prefecture had to be conducted exclusively in Italian. One year later, they went a step further: on 23 October 1923, the use of the Italian language became mandatory on all levels of federal, provincial, and local government, and on 28 October this was expanded to included signs and public notices. Posters, notices, tables, schedules, and the like were permitted in Italian only; photos, postcards, and maps had to show Italian place names. There were a number of instances of harassment and chicanery in the implementation of these regulations. Letters with a German address were not delivered; inns had to have German inscriptions removed from their china; a restauranteur in Gröden had to close his establishment because he forgot to have the word "*Warmwasser*" (warm water) removed from a pot in his kitchen. A farmer's wife had to remove the poppies from her garden because they bloomed in red and white. Since volunteer fire departments were particularly efficient and got to fires quickly, a Fascist official feared that they could be converted into a rapidly deployable fighting unit; therefore, they were then permitted to extinguish fires only after having obtained permission from him.

On 25 September 1925, Italian became the sole permissible language in courts of law; civil and criminal cases could thenceforth be tried in Italian only. Many South Tyroleans, however, could not speak Italian or had not mastered it yet and were thus in many instances forced to give false testimony. An interpreter was indeed permitted, but the defendant had to cover the cost himself, which was often impossible. Attorneys who spoke German among themselves were hit with a 5,000 Lire fine.

German judges had to decide to which of the other Italian provinces they wished to be transferred, since their native region offered no openings for them. Even German jurors were dismissed. The use of the German language in courts of law would remain a bone of contention for decades, even after World War II. The Italians insisted upon retaining the regulations that had been introduced by the Fascists, and were not ready to make concessions until the early 1990s.

In 1925, the process of eliminating communal autonomy began. A decree dated 16 April and published on 25 May revoked a community's right to name its own community secretary. A 1926 law removed freely elected mayors from office and replaced them with state-appointed mayors — the *Podestà*. Indeed, this measure applied to all of Italy, but had especially grave consequences for South Tyrol. The *Podestà* came almost exclusively from the "old" Italian provinces — above all, Lombardy and Piedmont — and could hardly speak German. Most did not take much of an interest in community affairs, performed their duties negligently if at all, often did not even possess the basic knowledge necessary to hold such an office, and not infrequently enriched themselves at the cost of the community. The "bridge between the man on the street and the authorities arrayed above them" had collapsed.

A law passed in May 1924 declared South Tyrol to be a fortified border region. All new construction and any and all architectural modifications or property transfers had to be authorized by the military authorities. The perfidious part of this was that such permission could also be revoked at any time, which would mean that the building would then have to be torn down. The military authorities could order the demolition of any building and annul any sales contract or lease. A prefect's decree dated 1 September 1926 declared South Tyrol a militarized region, a measure that served primarily to place the population under pressure.

Shutting Down the Press

German-language newspapers and magazines were still being published. They covered events and informed the populace as well as they could under the circumstances and were thus a particularly vexing thorn in the side of the Fascists, who then intensified the measures against them in early 1925. The assistant prefect of Bozen delivered the first blow on 8 January 1925; repeatedly citing "tendentious anti-Italian reportage," he made all German newspapers in South Tyrol subject to prepublication censorship. This applied to the dailies — *Der Landsmann*, the *Bozner Nachrichten* in Bozen, and the *Meraner Zeitung* in Meran — as well as the Bozen weekly *Volksbote*. On 20 January, *Der Landsmann* received its first warning. The editor-in-chief was accused of "biased" reporting, which was said to be preventing the "development of friendship and brotherhood between the two ethnic groups." Michael Gamper, editor-in-chief of the *Volksbote*, was warned on 20 February. According to the Press Law of 15 July 1923, a second warning could result in an order that the paper cease publication, and it did not take long for this second warning to arrive. Due to a violation of the 1923 Place Name Decree, *Der Landsmann* was warned again on 23 July, and had to shut down on 22 October 1925, as did the *Brixner Chronik*, the *Bozner Nachrichten* and the *Dolomiten*. A year later, the remaining papers suffered the same fate. Following a search of the Vogelweider Press' offices in Bozen and Meran, Guadagnini ordered the *Volksbote*, the *Volksblatt*, and the *Burggraefler* to cease publication. The *Meraner Zeitung* was the only paper that was — for a short time — still appearing. The most important "link connecting village to village and valley to valley was thus broken," Gamper wrote in a retrospective piece in the *Dolomiten* on 6 December 1952.

Behind these actions was the Fascists' intention to bring out a German-language daily of their own. They were able to bring this plan to fruition in the spring of 1926 after the *Meraner Zeitung* had been shut down and *Ellmenreich* Printers agreed to work together with them. The first issue of the Fascist *Alpenzeitung* came out on 2 March 1926, and *La Provincia di Bolzano*, the official organ of the Fascist Party of South Tyrol, began appearing on 22 April 1927. Meanwhile, Gamper, with the support of the Bishops of Brixen and Trient, had succeeded in obtaining permission to put out the *Dolomiten* and the *Volksbote* again. Thereafter, both publications appeared three times a week, though they were obliged to maintain a pro-regime editorial policy and were subject to strict censorship.

Italianization of the Schools

The School Law of 1 October 1923, the "Lex Gentile" named after Giovanni Gentile, the minister of education in Mussolini's first cabinet, was written to apply to Italy as a whole; nevertheless, in South Tyrol it led to the destruction of the German school system which was, indeed, the intended result. In the schools, Italianization advanced year by year. Each term, there was one fewer German class, until Prefect Alfredo Giarratana could report on 6 February 1928 that in 760 South Tyrolean classes, Italian was the only language of instruction, whereas supplementary instruction in German was still permitted in only thirty classes. The law affected 324 schools with 539 classes and 30,000 pupils in South Tyrol. German teachers were dismissed. The law also opened up the possibility of shutting down intermediate and secondary schools, which is exactly what happened in 1927-28. This law was "the most momentous and gravest de-nationalization decree of this time," the "death sentence" for German public education in South Tyrol. All German youngsters were from then on subjected to a cruel process of Italianization.

By 1924, the German Teachers College in Bozen was closed. On 3 May 1924, the Trient School Board ordered that the Italian language be used in German kindergartens, and the nursery schools then set up as a substitute for them were forcibly shut down. Additional decrees had to do with college degrees as well as intermediate and secondary schools; degrees from Austrian and German universities were thenceforth valid only after one year of study at an Italian university.

The Lex Gentile simultaneously began the systematic dismissal of German teachers. As the opportunity arose up to 1932, groups of teachers were terminated without compensation due to *"insufficienza didattica,"* or those who had earned a certificate of qualification in Italian were transferred to the south. In contrast, Italian teaching personnel were frequently lured to South Tyrol with false promises. On one hand, there was talk of the "miserable state of education of second-class citizens living out a wretched existence in a ghetto completely isolated from Roman culture"; on the other hand, government perks like a free apartment and mileage allowance were used to attract these Italian teachers. But for many of them, the stay in South Tyrol turned into a nightmare. Many were even surprised to hear what was to them a "foreign language" being spoken there. The teachers had to adhere strictly to the teaching plan with the mission of making "well-behaved little Italians" out of the children, irrespective of the linguistic, cultural, and social traditions of South Tyrol. Particularly in villages, they lived in isolation and were met with scorn, intolerance, and hostility, despite the fact that they were often better than their reputation. Most had not previously taught Italian as a second language, and had not had the slightest idea about the difficult situation their pupils faced. There was a stark contrast between what these children were hearing at home and what the teachers were trying to get across to them.

A new law dated 22 January 1925 that consolidated Italian school laws included an Article 169 that provided for the establishment of private schools. Nevertheless, this did not have much of an impact on South Tyrol. Textbooks and classroom space had to be authorized by the Trient School Board, which rarely happened. If permission was granted, school inspectors frequently revoked it without citing any grounds for their action. German private teachers had to undergo a language examination that most failed. Anyone who was employed as a private teacher had to inform the Italian village teacher when and where he was giving tutoring, so that the Italian teachers automatically became the supervisors of their German colleagues.

There remained only one subject whose instruction was in German: religion. Indeed, a royal decree of 13 November 1923 had ordered, "In all classes in which Italian has been established as the language of instruction, religious instruction must also be in Italian," but intervention by the Bishop of Brixen led to the maintenance of the *status quo* until 1925.

That same year, the Fascists sent a memorandum to Pope Pius XI demanding that the Church Italianize its institutions once and for all. They called for the removal of those elements that were hostile to the Italian nation from pastoral care and religious instruction. Furthermore, the Fascists demanded the Italianization of charitable institutions and the German religious orders as well as the suppression of the German language from the Church and, finally, the abolition of German religious instruction. The outcome was that, from then on, religious instruction during the final five years of mandatory school attendance had to be given in Italian, whereas, during the first three years, the German language was permitted to be used only as a means of explaining the Italian catechism. By the end of 1926, thirty-six South Tyrolean priests could no longer give catechism instruction.

When, during the 1926-27 school year, religious instruction was to be Italianized once and for all, the clergy, on the advice of Brixen Bishop Johannes Raffl, resigned *en masse* from teaching. In the spring of 1928, the Vatican then authorized parishes to provide instruction using the German language outside of the schools, which had previously not been standard practice in South Tyrol. These parish schools that held classes in Church buildings or apartment houses deserve a great deal of credit for maintaining the German language in the face of considerable problems. Instruction was kept under strict surveillance; report cards were often confiscated immediately after they were passed out. Contrary to regulations, a bit of language instruction was also given, though this was not looked upon very kindly by the Vatican, which wanted to avoid any sort of controversy with Mussolini during the negotiation of the Lateran Treaties.

These Lateran Treaties of 11 February 1929 guaranteed the continued existence of four of the Church's private boarding schools for boys, including both of its German-language seminaries: the Vinzentinum in Brixen and the Johanneum in the village Dorf Tyrol.

Catacomb Schools

In the area of education, the South Tyroleans put up resistance in the form of "catacomb schools." Here, Canon Michael Gamper, long-time editor of the *Volksbote,* played the decisive role. Immediately after the passage of the Lex Gentile, he published the following in his paper:

> What should be done now? In addition to the loss of German schools, are we to lose our national customs and traditions as well? Those who hold power today would like that. A high administration official justified this measure with the explanation that the government must make the effort to raise a young generation of Italians in our land as quickly as possible. Could they possibly succeed? Let's hope that our people are capable of preventing it! Now we have to imitate the early Christians. When they were no longer safe from persecution while holding religious services in public, they withdrew to the privacy of their own homes. . . . And when they were not safe from harassment even there, they found refuge among the dead in the underground burial chambers, in the catacombs.

Michael Gamper became the driving force behind clandestine schools that were then set up, and which would go down in the history of South Tyrol as "catacomb schools." On 27 November 1924 in the *Volksbote*, he made it clear what had to be done: "Until our fight to re-establish German schools is won, the only alternative left to us is home schooling." His message was understood by all and motivated families, unemployed teachers, and priests to dedicate their efforts to setting up clandestine schools.

On 7 March 1922, Gamper was made chairman of the Tyrolean People's Party; this subsequently enabled him to establish contacts in Austria and Germany that would ensure outside help in setting up these emergency schools. German schoolbooks and necessary teaching materials then made their way across the border through secret channels. It was mostly students from Innsbruck and South Tyrol who were involved in these efforts; many were members of *Nibelungen*, a German nationalist association, and later of the Nazi

Völkischer Kampfring Südtirols (VKS, or People's Action Group of South Tyrol). Often, sacristies, parish houses, and churches were used as hiding places for these items before they were distributed to South Tyrolean pupils.

In 1923, the Fascists ban the German language in South Tyrol. From then on, Italian is to be the only language of instruction. The South Tyroleans put up resistance in the form of clandestine schools, called "catacomb schools," imitating the early Christians in ancient Rome.

In the 1920s and early 1930s, primarily Austrian primers, storybooks, and collections of fables were employed; the three-part Zeller Fibel and Walter Dietno's primer *Unseren Kindern* were widely used. Books of fairy tales and songs were clandestinely supplied by German cultural societies. Although Gamper made every effort to use textbooks that did not propagate German irredentism, it is certainly reasonable to presume that the teaching materials provided by the German cultural societies enabled concepts of the mythically superior peasantry's rootedness to the soil and other *völkisch*-totalitarian clichés to also, here and there, seep into the instruction provided by the network of catacomb schools. In this sense, the catacomb schools were not merely Catholic-conservative in their orientation, but were imparted with a more or less German nationalist tinge as well.

For organizational and administrative reasons, South Tyrol was divided into three districts: Bozen and its suburbs, Brixen including the upper Eisacktal and Pustertal, and Meran including Burggrafenamt and Vinschgau. One of the chief problems was finding teachers. Young girls who had not yet learned a trade were approached. They were selected by the village clergymen and given training to prepare them for the job.

In July and August of 1925 in a top secret training program disguised as a sewing course held in Bozen, the first group of twenty-five girls from the *Unterland* were taught the barebones skills to be teachers. A second course was organized in Grado with the girls pretending to be vacationers. This had to be terminated prematurely, though, and transferred to the Marieninternat, a boarding school in Bozen, where instruction could be completed without further interruption. Thereafter, courses were offered throughout South Tyrol, most of them under the aegis of the Church. Then in 1931, courses were held in Munich.

These activities did not escape the attention of the Fascists. On 25 November, Prefect Guadagnini stated:

> The exposure of a considerable number of secret German schools, especially in the area between Bolzano and Salorno, proves that there exists in Alto Adige what is tantamount to a resistance organization that is responsible for recruiting teachers, setting up schools, and providing the necessary financing. In this matter, to which I attribute a particularly high degree of political significance, I expect the utmost vigilance, alacrity, and energy.[8]

Legislation dated 6 November 1926 launched the Fascist counteroffensive. A campaign that included searches of private residences, interrogations, maltreatment, confiscation of German schoolbooks, warnings, imprisonment, and deportation went on for years in an effort to destroy the catacomb schools; two of them died after returning from exile. The brutality with which the Italian authorities went about this business provoked fear and terror throughout the land. It also elicited outrage in Austria and Germany, where there were also numerous manifestations of solidarity with the South Tyroleans and their fate.

Despite the idealism of and sacrifices by those involved, the clandestine instruction could be carried on only in a very primitive, inadequate way. One reason for this was that barns, attics, cellars, and farmhouse kitchens had to serve as classrooms; another was that the opportunities for proper instruction were severely limited. German instruction being given parallel to public school instruction meant a heavy burden for the pupils in that what they were being taught in the Italian schools, especially in social studies and history, was the exact opposite of what they were learning in the underground schools. The South Tyrolean journalist Claus Gatterer later spoke of this lack of identity on the part of the children: "We were torn, and our cover-up was lies — at home, we lied about school; in school, we lied about home and about ourselves." In the public schools, the situation became chaotic as Italian teachers left the region of their own accord. The effect of the frequent personnel changes that resulted was that some third graders could not even read or write. Illiteracy rose dramatically.

Due to the courage, discretion, and solidarity of many individuals, the Fascist authorities never succeeded in wiping out the German provisional schools. They were not discontinued until 1940, when it was once again officially permissible to use German. For the Italian Fascists, though, it was almost inconceivable that, in spite of the wide-ranging and rigorous measures taken to suppress the schools, the German language still managed to survive, although the reasons for this were quite obvious.

Additional Measures

These fascist denationalization measures had an impact on virtually every aspect of South Tyrolean life. In the spring of 1927, the Fascist's national sport commission *Ente nazionale per educazione fisica* was founded; its job was to supervise local sports organizations to prevent anti-national propaganda. New regulations were continually being issued for business and public facilities. Beginning in July 1928, hotels, restaurants, and taverns had to display pictures of the royal couple and *Il Duce*. Whoever refused to comply and displayed a "lack of patriotism" could count on paying the price: in most cases, closure of the business. Bills and statements of account had to be either in Italian or bilingual. At the same time, stricter measures were instituted against individuals "who had made themselves *personae non gratae* or seemed to be dangerous." According to Reut-Nicolussi, in 1927 approximately 100 individuals were issued special ID cards that had been provided for in the Police Law of 1925 for "dangerous or suspicious persons," and were thus placed under *de facto* police surveillance. In September 1927, Reut-Nicolussi's office was closed, and in October those of the South Tyrolean Representatives Karl Tinzl and Paul von Sternbach. These offices had played an important role in enabling these legislators to work together with their constituents. The reason for the closures was simply "anti-Italian propaganda." Public libraries had to make available the exact same number of Italian and German books; kiosks and cafés had to offer as many Italian newspapers and magazines as German ones.

The Fascists' attitude is very clearly revealed by the provisions of Decree Nr. 7622 of 16 November 1927. In it, Umberto Ricci, the first prefect of the newly created Province of Bozen, banned all German gravestone inscriptions, which henceforth had to be in Italian. The Fascist Party's secretary for the Province of Bozen played this down in his remarks in the 28 February 1928 issue of *Popolo d'Italia*: "The Italian Government will not lay even a finger on the past; our mission is the future."

In an interview with the *Pétit Parisien*, Mussolini alluded to a project that incorporated all aspects of Fascist policies toward South Tyrol: construction of an ammonia factory in the vicinity of Sinich and the founding of Borgo Vittoria. Here, Fascist industrial policy — the first and (for years) only example of which had been the Sinich project — was designed to meld together the exploitation of hydroelectric power; agriculture, including "domestic colonization"; and the whole business of subsidies and credits, as well as the policy of Italianization via the "majorification" of the South Tyroleans.

An additional instrument of Italianization was the *Ente di Rinascita Agraria per le Tre Venezie*, the so-called ERA, which had been founded in 1921 and became autonomous in 1929. Its mission was to take over operations from farmers who were forced to give up during the Depression. The intention behind this was to acquire as much land and other real estate as possible in order to thus facilitate the migration of Italians to the region. This effort was aimed at the conquest of the soil, the *conquista del suolo*. Actually, a similar development had begun to emerge even before this; however, the attempt to gain influence over South Tyrolean farmers had failed by 1926. Indeed, the Italians succeeded — though not without ignominious "assistance" from the Germans' own ranks — in subordinating the South Tyrolean Farmers' Association to the Fascists' Syndicate of Farmers, although this transformation remained rather a formal act since the political leadership of the farmers went over to the German association. In a second phase, the attempt was made to deprive the Farmers' Association of financial support.

In South Tyrol, most communities had their own *Raiffeisenkasse*, which provided commercial credit to farmers, agricultural organizations and co-ops. The headquarters of this organization was the Agricultural Central Bank in Bozen, which oversaw a total of 136 local *Raiffeisenkasse* branches. In October 1926, thirty-six Fascists from Trient broke up the annual meeting of the Central Bank and prevented the election of a new board of directors. The next day, Antonio de Steffanini was appointed supervisor of the organization. The Fascists had thus achieved their aim: a purely German financial institution had been placed under compulsory Italian administration. One year later, *Raiffeisenkasse* had to close its doors due to insolvency. All that remained were the savings banks in Bozen, Brixen, Meran, Bruneck, St. Ulrich, Schlanders, and Sterzing; their Italianization proceeded step by step. Legislation from 1928 mandated that there be only one savings bank per province. At first, the merger of the savings banks in Bozen, Meran, and Bruneck was ordered — with a government-appointed president. This was consistent with the general Fascist policy of fostering bank concentration. It was not until 1935 that a South Tyrolean Savings Bank was founded.

Royal Decree Nr. 2525 dated 4 November 1928 must also be assessed in the context of the "conquest of the soil." It invalidated the Austrian Civil Law Code that was still legally valid in South Tyrol and introduced Italian civil law in its entirety as of 1 July 1929. This also set aside the Tyrolean Farm Rule (last modified in 1900) that prevented the subdivision of farms and mandated unitary inheritance. The regime wanted to break up parcels in order to make economic survival impossible for South Tyrolean farmers, and thus to destroy the most important segment of the population that had *de facto* control over the entire primary sector of the economy.

The Fascists did not achieve their goal, primarily because the farmers, despite their lack of a legal basis, succeeded in circumventing the problem through their wills or *inter vivos* transfers, and stood by the institution of impartibility. Of 12,000 unitary farms, only 6.2 percent were subdivided prior to reintroduction of the Farm Rule in the context of the First Autonomy Statute in 1948.

All in all, the ERA's bottom line was negative. It took over sixty farms in 1931, ninety-eight in 1932, 190 in 1933, 263 in 1934 and, finally, 350 in 1939, some of which were resold to Italian farmers. Self-help initiatives on the part of South Tyrolean farmers and aid from "abroad" — Germany and Austria — had prevented even more farms from changing hands.

The Fascist "Victory Monument"

"An arrogant demonstration of the Italianization of South Tyrol" is how the German historian Rudolf Lill quite accurately characterizes the Victory Monument in Bozen. Of all the structures the Fascists put up, this one has provoked the most violent differences of opinion, and still does to this day. The Italian Chamber of Deputies passed the resolution to construct a victory monument in Bozen on 10 February 1926. The monument was not only intended to represent the Italian victory over the enemy from beyond the Alps; rather, Mussolini also wanted a symbol for the process of Italianization he had been pushing forward, and this was to become an integral element in the new city planning being done in Bozen in conjunction with the colonization of South Tyrol. The *Duce* himself sketched a design for this grandiose undertaking, and also appointed the members of the commission responsible for it. Tolomei suggested erecting the monument at a highly visible spot where the South Tyrolean valleys converge — in particular, near the Talfer Bridge on the very spot where the already completed exterior shell of the memorial to the Austrian *Kaiserjaeger* troops who fell during World War I stood. That structure was dynamited and removed, and the Victory Monument was put up on the same spot, yet another humiliation of the South Tyroleans, the Austrians, and the Germans.

An arrogant demonstration of the Italianization of South Tyrol: the Fascist "Victory Monument" in Bozen, built from 1926 to 1928.

Marcello Piacentini, one of the regime's favored architects, was commissioned to design the monument. He expressed his thanks to Mussolini in the following words, "I wish to assure Your Excellency that I will use all of my power and enthusiasm for this work of such enormous political significance. It is my intention to create a truly fascist monument, to employ the power of art and the symbols of Romanness to underscore the eternal vigor of our people." All of Italy was enthused by the plan. A collection drive exceeded even the most optimistic expectations; in a very short time, three million Lire were raised, and even Mussolini himself chipped in with a personal contribution.

The laying of the cornerstone on 12 July 1926, the tenth anniversary of the execution of Cesare Battisti, became a political demonstration. (When in 1915 Italy entered the war against Austria, Cesare Battisti, a member of the Austrian parliament from the Trentino, fled the country and entered the Italian army. In July 1916 he was captured by the Austrians, accused of high treason, and a few days later hanged.) Participants included King Victor Emanuel III, Marshalls Luigi Cadorna and Pietro Badoglio, Ministers Pietro Fedele and Pietro Cavallaro, and Tolomei among others. Prince

Bishop Celestino Endrici of Trient consecrated the endeavor. Enclosed within the cornerstone was piece a parchment on which had been written Gabriele D'Annunzio's lucubration on victory, the gist of which was that this monument was meant to display the power of the Italian state before the eyes of the South Tyroleans.

As construction neared completion, Minister Fedele selected the Latin inscription for the front side of the monument facing the city, words which still adorn it to this day: "HIC PATRIAE FINES SISTE SIGNA HINC CETEROS EXCOLUIMUS LINGUA LEGIBUS ARTIBUS" ("Here are the borders of the fatherland. Put down our weapons" [i.e. stop our advance]. From here, we brought to the others language, laws, and arts.) Each column is a fasces, the projecting axe blade of which replaces the column's capital. Along the row of rectangular stone blocks that comprises the main façade facing the city is the sculpture *"Vittoria Sagittaria"* firing an arrow toward the north. This is meant as an admonition to Austria that the political intransigence of the Fascist state with regard to South Tyrol would never soften.

The official dedication of the Victory Monument took place on 12 July 1928, after Austrian Chancellor Ignaz Seipel had declared South Tyrol to be solely Italy's domestic affair. Those present, as at the laying of the foundation stone, included the King, the Duke of Aosta, the Count of Turin, and the Duke of Abruzzi as well as high-ranking Fascist dignitaries. Endrici once again gave the blessing of the Church. The Fascist Minister Giovanni Giurati, representing Mussolini, declared that the monument was being dedicated

> on the borders of the fatherland, in this city founded by Drusus that had preserved its Italian character intact until the dawn of the previous century, and which will very quickly be freed of every effort to conceal that. The rope around Cesare Battisti's neck will eternally deliver a tragic, indisputable answer to those on the other side of the Alps who still advocate the cause of the usurper. It will forever state that the geographers and history determine the territorial rights of a nation and that the border demarcated by a strand of mountain peaks . . . will never be permitted to be changed. A great people of sober and astute workers and soldiers cannot tolerate even the discussion of borders that have been instituted by God. It cannot permit the

tiny minorities that have migrated into a few provinces during the past centuries to serve as a pretext for bold claims.⁹

The monument is a medium communicating a number of contradictory messages. Most contradictory is the statue of Cesare Battisti, who, as was widely known, did not advocate the annexation of South Tyrol to Italy. The fact that the monument was not named after Battisti as planned is attributable to the resistance of Battisti's family. Unlike a few other Fascist shrines, the Victory Monument was not destroyed after 1945; only an inscription glorifying Mussolini was removed. The monument has repeatedly served Italian nationalists as a setting to promote hate and discord; especially notorious were the wreath laying ceremonies every 4 November, the "Day of the Army," although these are not taking place any more.

Besides the Victory Monument in Bozen, the Fascists in the 1930s also erected "their" monuments elsewhere in South Tyrol, either precisely in those places where South Tyrolean monuments previously had been torn down, as in the case of the Victory Monument, or in their immediate vicinity, such as the *Alpini* Monument on what was then Savoy Square in Meran, or the ten-ton *Alpini* Monument built in 1938 in Bruneck, and depicting an *Alpini* soldier in a hooded cloak. Because of the hood (*Kapuze* in German), it was referred to as "*Kapuziner-Wastl*" in South Tyrolean vernacular. In 1944, a German tank knocked it off its plinth; in 1951 (!) it was reconstructed by the Italians. As the situation in South Tyrol deteriorated, the first dynamite attack on 20 February 1959 targeted this statue; on 2 December 1966 a second such explosion demolished it. A few hours after the attack, representatives of various Italian veterans organizations in South Tyrol convened and sent the following telegram to the Italian government:

> Outraged and with their innermost feelings injured most grievously, proud of the symbols and traditions of the purest glory of heroic love of country, and inspired by the will to strike back, the South Tyrolean *Alpini*, as worthy representatives of the great Italian community, stand in lonely dismay and desolation before the ruins of the *Alpini* Monument in Bruneck that was brutally destroyed by high explosives. Vowing never to allow their proud wills to be broken, determined to go to any

lengths, constantly prepared, they cry out in a stentorian voice *"Basta"* [that's enough]!

Minister of the Interior Paolo Emilio Taviani provided 10 million Lire to repair the monument, commissioning for the job the same man who had produced it in 1938. The South Tyrolean People's Party came out emphatically against reconstructing the monument. On 30 July 1967, the provisionally restored monument was unveiled, this time dedicated to "all the troops who had fought in the Alps." On 30 June 1968, the repaired monument was removed, shipped to Cuneo, and set up on the grounds of the army base there. An identical new monument was installed in its place. From throughout northern Italy, 10,000 *Alpini* veterans came to take part in the grandiose dedication ceremony. Mario Barello, the provincial secretary of the National Association of Alpine Soldiers, declared that the monument "was meant to inspire to loyal and honorable deeds [all those] who truly love this land."

Yet another monument was erected in 1938, this time in aluminium: the equestrian statue in Waidbruck that bore a clear resemblance to Mussolini and was referred to by locals as the "aluminium *Duce*." The inscription read *"Al genio del fascismo,"* and was revised to *"Al genio del lavoro italiano"* in 1945. Tyrolean "freedom fighters" blew up this monument on 30 January 1961. Prime Minister Amintore Fanfani instructed the minister for public works to have it rebuilt, but this project was then allowed to die a quiet death.

The 1920s also witnessed the construction of "charnel houses" of sorts (*Beinhaeuser*), where bodies were not stored, but skulls and bones of Italian soldiers were put on display behind glass, giving the impression that they had fallen in their fight for South Tyrol. This constituted yet another gross distortion of history since not a single Italian soldier had made it as far as South Tyrol during World War I.

The Destruction of Tyrolean Monuments

If one wants to rob a minority of its identity, then one must also deprive it of its symbols. This is exactly what happened in South Tyrol. The Italians had created their symbol, the Victory Monument; then, their aim was to remove or destroy the most important South

Tyrolean monuments that had a symbolic character: the Walther Monument, the Laurin Fountain, and the Bozen Museum. The Walther Monument had been dedicated on 15 September 1898. On that occasion, the chairman of the organizing committee uttered the wish that, so long as even the tiniest grain of the stone remained intact, Bozen would remain "a city infused with German spirit." (At that time, Bozen had 10,000 inhabitants with 10 percent Italians; today the figures are 100,000 with roughly 75 percent Italians.) Mayor Julius Perathoner vowed in the name of the city that the monument was emblematic of the desire to preserve eternally this German feeling and the loyalty of the people to the Austrian Double Eagle. This was why Tolomei demanded its removal. In 1934 in the *Archivio per l'Alto Adige*, he wrote:

> Walther von der Vogelweide remains the notorious symbol, the symbol of Germanness dominating South Tyrol, a symbol based on a flagrant error, since, in the meantime, it has been acknowledged even by German literary criticism that the poet was born in the Danube Basin and not in Alto Adige. Thus, it was by means of fraud and violence that this pan-Germanic symbol was erected on the main square of Bozen, where it remains to this day.
>
> [Former German Foreign Minister Gustav] Stresemann says that it is irrelevant whether he was a great poet or a minor one; be that as it may, he is the symbol of the German nation on the southern slope of the Alps. And the countless articles written by the proponents of irredentism in Tyrol, Bavaria, and Berlin focus on this very stone, look toward the city it occupies and that is still referred to as the Walther City: Bolzano, the City of Walther!
>
> . . . Therefore, we have always demanded and continue to demand that this phony monument be removed and presented to one of the German cities that wish to have it. The return of this stone to its fatherland beyond the Brenner means an intellectual Locarno, a voluntary abnegation of Germanness, the spontaneous recognition of the eternal boundary between the two peoples. Otherwise, it ought to be removed in an honorable

manner to the grounds of the museum as a remembrance of days gone by. But on the main square of Bozen, the city founded by Drusus, Walther's place should be taken by the Latin hero who was the first to open up the valleys of the Etschland to civilized life.

The return of Drusus is the return of Rome!

On 8 August 1935, the *Podestà* (Mayor) of Bozen decided to relocate the monument to a secluded park; the official justification was to allow for better traffic flow. Drusus never did return, but the Walther Monument did: since 1981 it has been back in its original location.

In 1933, persons unknown destroyed the Laurin Fountain in Bozen, a work by the sculptor Andrae Kompatscher dating from 1907 that depicts Dietrich of Bern's fight against the Dwarf King Laurin. According to legend, Laurin held a princess prisoner in his rose garden. After his defeat by Dietrich von Bern — the historical Theoderich — the rose garden turned to stone, which explains the red color that the massif of the same name assumes at sundown. In the 1930s more than ever, this legend expressed the intimate relationship of the people of Bozen with their mountain landscape and became an allegory for the idea of homeland, for a feeling of belonging to this place where men and women experienced this spectacle of nature and continue to do so. Just like Walther, Laurin as well was endowed with a national meaning — Dietrich was said to stand for Germanness that vanquished the Italians. At least that is how Tolomei saw it:

> And something else that should be made to disappear from the parks along the Talfer is that intolerable, misshapen figure of the German warrior preparing to crush the little Latin people of the mountains. The Honorable Mr. [Pietro] Rava, who came Bozen to attend the scholarly conference, pointed out in his marvelous speech in the Theater that Theoderich, the king of the Goths who built imposing Romanic architecture in Ravenna and had been thoroughly imbued with Roman culture, was, in historical reality, someone quite different than that insulting figure in Bozen – the German warrior who stoops to crush King

Laurin. The meaning of this is none other than to juxtapose mighty Germany to us small, lowly people. To tolerate such a thing in a public park of an Italian city means that one is either unaware of the facts or seeking to conceal the affront.

In the 1980s, the monument was restored, and has stood since then on the square in front of the *Landhaus,* the South Tyrolean parliament building.

Another highly symbolic site was the Bozen Museum. The Museum Society was founded in 1882 by a group of the city's prominent citizens; according to its charter, the museum was to engage in the cultivation of local arts and crafts and the display of German and Tyrolean traditions. The museum was financed by the city. In 1902, the City Council decided to construct a new museum in what is now *Museumstrasse.* Tolomei raised the first Italian flag here in 1918, and made the museum the headquarters of his Commission for the Language and Culture of the Oberetsch. He called for the Italianization of the museum, which he regarded as one of the strongholds of Germanness. In his opinion, its purpose had been to give visitors from all over the world the impression that the area had been German since time immemorial and would always remain so. The objects exhibited were said to have been arranged accordingly. Over the following years, though, the museum did succeed in preserving a certain degree of autonomy. It was not until 1934 that the *Podestà* decided to tear down the museum tower — in order to avoid spoiling the view of the *Rosengarten* massif, as the official explanation put it. Actually, the aim was to Italianize the building's exterior, and to carry on the medieval custom of victorious families razing the towers of those they had subjugated.

The Industrial Zone in Bozen

Today, if one travels to Bozen by car and approaches on the turnpike from the north, one sees on the left side the immense industrial zone that has constituted the most lasting change to the structure of the city. This industrial zone and the recruitment of Italian laborers to work there were designed to change the relationship between the German-speaking and Italian-speaking segments of the population in favor of the latter. The number of

Italians employed in the industrial zone rose from zero in 1936 to 7,000 in 1942-43, and by an additional 12,000 by 1947. Most of the immigrants came from neighboring Italian regions (above all Veneto, as well as Belluno, Vicenza, Padua, Rovigo, and Verona) and from the adjacent districts of Friuli and Lombardy as well as Trentino. The fact that almost all of these workers came from the same area was attributable to intentional planning on the part of the regime, which aimed to further the formation of a linguistic and regional identity among the Italians settled in Bozen. The fact that this did not succeed is chiefly attributable to the tremendous historical and social diversity of these different peoples despite their having come from the same regions, and that the authorities were unable to regulate the influx as perfectly as they had envisioned.

The "Measures for the Industrial Development of the Community of Bozen," as the legislation was named, were announced in September 1934. On 20 February 1935, leading Italian industrialists and top-ranking politicians from the Province of Bozen gathered in the Palazzo Venezia in Rome, where Mussolini informed them about the government's plans and gave the major industries of Lombardy and Piemont the directive to set up plants in Bozen. In order to make the establishment of branches in an economically unattractive area like Bozen somewhat more palatable to these Italian industrialists, a decree dated 9 May 1935 instituted preferential tax treatment and fee exemptions for the workers. In the fall of 1935, workers began bulldozing the industrial zone. To make way for construction, 50,000 fruit trees were felled shortly before harvest, which especially embittered the locals. At this time, Mussolini visited the construction site. A year later, as compensation for the industrial zone's unfavorable geographical location, the government reduced railroad transportation rates for freight deliveries to and from the south — thus, discounts for the purchase of raw materials and the shipment of finished goods. A 130-kilometer long "free ride" zone was instituted — exactly the distance from Bozen to the junction of the Brenner line in the Po Basin. The lines leading north — the Bozen-Brenner line with its spur to Innichen, and the Bozen-Mals line — were expressly excluded from these discount rates. The first factories, subsidiary plants of major Italian firms, were opened by 1937-38: an aluminium works of the Montecatini Corporation, a fiber board works of the Feltrinelli-Masonite Corporation of Milan, a magnesium works of the Società Italiana per il Magnesio (1939), the Falck Group's Acciaierie di Bolzano Steel Works, and the Viberti Auto Body Plant of the Lancia Group headquartered in Turin. This last-named firm also set up the Lancia Works, the largest factory in the industrial zone. The original plan called for only replacement parts and castings for automobiles to be produced there; later, they retooled to allow from complete production of cars and trucks. The workforce increased accordingly from 400 in 1936 and 600 in 1940 to 2,000 in 1942 and later to 6,000. The plant could produce up to 200 trucks a month.

Most of the operations that were set up in Bozen required tremendous amounts of energy in their production processes, and energy could be had rather cheaply in Bozen. The Kardaun Power Plant provided electricity; coal no longer came by ship from England, but rather by rail from Germany. Nevertheless, this by no means disproves the contention that Bozen was a site that simply did not make economic sense for a number of the plants. This applied in particular to the aluminium works, which had to transport its raw materials from Porto Marghera (Venice) to Bozen and, in turn, ship the finished metal back there again.

For the workers and their families, giant housing projects and quasi-country-style developments — the so-called four-family *semirurali* patterned after the house in which Mussolini was born in Predappio — were built on the right bank of the Eisack directly across from the new industrial zone. The workers' housing was put up quickly between 1937 and 1939 parallel to the construction of the industrial zone. The housing was very simple; each of the little homes had a garden of about 100 m^2 designed to preserve the recollection of the land, since most of the occupants of the *semirurali* were peasants who had been forced by the recession to give up farming and become laborers. The houses were cold and damp, and in the entire development there were no places for socializing or recreational facilities. Nevertheless, these *semirurali* have tremendous significance in the collective consciousness of the Italians of South Tyrol; they are a point with which they can identify. Since then, they have given way to modern apartment complexes. One unit still stands, and there are plans to turn it into a museum.

Through the establishment of the Bozen Industrial Zone, "which can be regarded as the actual impetus behind the inundation of South

Tyrol with those speaking a different language, Fascism left behind a legacy that had an impact upon almost all areas of life long after the end of World War II." At least in this regard, Giuseppe Mastromattei, prefect since 1933, did a very thorough job.

IV. 1939: Between Fascism and National Socialism — The Option

The Nazi *Völkischer Kampfring Südtirols* (VKS)

In the meantime, an interesting development had begun to emerge on the South Tyrolean side. In 1926, the legally constituted political leadership of the South Tyroleans, the German Association, had been outlawed. At the time of its dissolution, there had already existed so-called youth groups that would go on to become the nuclei from which the National Socialist movement in South Tyrol would develop. They merged in 1927-28 to form the Gau-Jugend-Rat (GJR, District Youth Council). This body was politically oriented from the very start, and not exclusively concerned with culture or sport. It would later produce many of the leading members of the Nazi association in the area, the Völkischer Kampfring Suedtirols (VKS, The People's Action Group of South Tyrol), including such committed National Socialists as Robert Helm and Norbert Mumelter. Therefore, the GJR can be seen as a forerunner to the VKS. Up to 1933, though, the GJR could not assume leadership in South Tyrol; this was primarily attributable to the resistance of the old politicians from the German Association, who increasingly regarded this as a threat to their own leadership role, as well as to the oppositional stance of the Catholic Action, which feared the loss of its monopoly on youth work. Up to this point, there was basically no tension between the German Association and the GJR. That changed after Adolf Hitler took power in January 1933, when the GJR was swept along in the Nazis' wake and took the decisive step in the direction of the Nazi movement. At a mass meeting held at Haselburg near Bozen on 18 June 1933, the decision was made to found an organization based on the *"Führer* principle." Three students, Norbert Mumelter, Kurt Heinricher and Robert Helm, as well as Rolf Hillebrand, who until then had headed the GJR and was now appointed "first district leader of the movement," had been instrumental in paving the way. The movement's name, which had still been Südtiroler Heimatfront (South Tyrolean homefront) in 1933, was changed to Völkischer Kampfring Südtirols in early 1934. The very name was indicative of its program. In accordance with the Führer principle, its organizational structure was strictly hierarchical, and the key elements of its platform were oriented on the Nationalsozialistische Deutsche Arbeiterpartei (NSDAP or German National Socialist Workers' Party). Its self-proclaimed goal was the "saturation of the South Tyrolean people with the National Socialist *Weltanschauung*." In 1935, Peter Hofer, a master tailor from Bozen and a product of the Catholic Youth League, took over as head of the VKS (in December 1943 he was killed in an Allied bombing raid on Bozen).

While Nazi propaganda succeeded in chalking up ever-greater successes in South Tyrol, Fascist politics *per se* fell into a deepening crisis. None of the measures in the areas of language, schools, and public administration was able to make Italians out of German-speaking South Tyroleans. The realization that National Socialism was attracting more and more supporters was just one more reason to revive old projects designed to further mass immigration of Italians from the other provinces to South Tyrol that had been only partially implemented. It was in this context in 1934 that Rome developed the idea of setting up an industrial zone in Bozen.

Under these circumstances, the referendum in the Saarland on reunification with the German Reich that was held on 13 January 1935 — with 90.7 percent voting for Germany — had a particularly powerful impact, although Hitler had had absolutely nothing to do with the date of the vote. In South Tyrol, the number of listeners tuned to German radio stations on this day was especially high. Bonfires were lit high in the mountains; Nazi symbols and irredentist mottos like *"heute die Saar — wir übers Jahr"* ("Today the Saar, next year it's our turn") began to appear. Many hoped that what had happened in the Saarland would happen in South Tyrol too: "Perhaps the day will come for us as well when we will go to the polls and joyously cast our votes for the German fatherland," or "We are waiting for the day when we will also be able to take part in a vote to determine our own fate." Indeed, that day would come soon – though it would be quite different than what the South Tyroleans had hoped for and expected.

The Anschluß of Austria

The events surrounding the Anschluß of Austria in March 1938 raised the self-esteem of the South Tyroleans to an undreamt of extent: the *Führer* would show those Dagos! Gleefully and as a sign of confirmation of the people's long-standing faith, the rumor circulated that Mussolini would give Hitler South Tyrol as a "wedding present" to celebrate their new alliance. With German men at the Brenner Pass in March 1938, jubilation and elation, hopes and expectations were boundless in South Tyrol. A new age seemed to have dawned; the years of persistent waiting appeared to have paid off. It seemed to be only a matter of time until the *Führer* would also bring South Tyrol "home into the Reich," and the new border would be drawn in the vicinity of Salurn. Just as the illegal Nazis in Austria had triumphed, the illegal Nazis in South Tyrol would soon prevail as well. Enthusiasm knew no bounds, and only the smallest handful of South Tyroleans were willing or able to accept Hitler's well-known, frequently reiterated and confirmed renunciation of any claim to South Tyrol at face value — namely, as the final word on the subject. Up to this point, many had just not been willing to accept this fact, and interpreted it as simply a tactical maneuver to throw Mussolini off the track. Mussolini obviously saw things that way too — at least, the Fascists' South Tyrol policy during the 1930s with its expansion of military installations in that region could be interpreted that way.

On 11 March 1938, Hitler solemnly promised Mussolini once again that, whatever the consequences of upcoming events would be, he had established a clear border with France, and would now establish an equally clear one with Italy. "It is the Brenner. I did not reach this decision in 1938, but rather immediately after the Great War, and I have never made a secret of it." For once, he had told the truth. South Tyrol would not become a stumbling block between him and the *Duce*. He had made this clear several times before, and he had made it clear that the partition of Tyrol after World War I had been a Jewish conspiracy. He had nothing to do with that.

How did VKS regional chief Peter Hofer react? He made it clear to his comrades that the *Führer* now stood at the Brenner with the greatness and power of the consolidated German people, and the faith in and commitment to the fight to secure Germany's southernmost border was positively immeasurable. He said that there was now just one single great German Reich stretching from the Alps to the Baltic that would soon have unchallenged predominance in Central Europe. Accordingly, it now played "an inconsiderable role that the *Führer*, in order to prevent a concerted attack by all major European powers, was forced to give Mussolini assurances about the Brenner border. As painful as this fact is for us, it cannot detract from our joy at this much greater event — the unity of Germany."[10] Disillusionment set in for some during Hitler's speech in Rome on 7 May 1938, in which he once again made it clear that it was his "unshakeable will and his mandate to the German people to look upon the Alpine border established by nature as forever inviolable."

The reaction of Norbert Mumelter, who heard Hitler's address, already provided an early indication of the direction in which the VKS was headed. The "mandate of the *Führer*" initially sent Mumelter's feelings crashing to the ground, but then he caught hold of himself; he got a grip on the situation and formulated what was for him the "ultimate rationale," namely, "For Greater Germany, one must be prepared to sacrifice even one's homeland," as he wrote in his diary.[11]

The Hitler-Mussolini Agreement

In 1939, the South Tyroleans would be sacrificed to the alliance of the two dictators, Hitler and Mussolini. They were confronted by the choice of either opting for German citizenship, which was connected with being resettled out of their hereditary homeland, or deciding to retain Italian citizenship, which came with the threat of no longer being able to lay claim to any kind of protection for their national customs and traditions. The bitter alternative was either to betray one's Germanness by staying or to betray one's homeland by going; to resettle to the German Reich or a territory that Germany had conquered, or to remain in the increasingly Italianized homeland under the constant threat of being resettled "south of the Po." The overwhelming majority of the South Tyroleans (approximately 86 percent) became "goers"; the "stayers" were simultaneously accused of treason. The Option was no doubt the most painful chapter of South Tyrol's history; it is a topic that was taboo for decades thereafter and will probably forever remain a problematical issue. Emotions have hardly subsided to this day, and they make it hard to come to an impartial assessment. The questions connected with it are tough to resolve.

Those who seek the answer solely in the events of the period from June/July to December 1939 and who indiscriminately characterize the majority of those South Tyroleans who opted for Germany as Nazis and traitors to their homeland, calling the referendum an unambiguous declaration of allegiance to Hitler and the Third Reich, are on the wrong track in that they are oversimplifying a complex situation, although this should not be construed to mean that there were no convinced, fanatical Nazis in South Tyrol in those days. There were indeed, and they helped to plunge an entire people into the most profound despair. Things are much more complicated than this, however, and there are no simple answers. If the results of the Option show anything, then they show how successful Nazi propaganda was.

On 23 June 1939 in Berlin, the agreement was reached that Bernardo Attolico, the Italian ambassador in Berlin, described with consummate cynicism as "an act of extraordinary political wisdom." What was on the line was the fate of South Tyrol, and after two hours of negotiation, the Germans and Italians were fundamentally in agreement about resettlement of the South Tyroleans. "Human resource reallocation" was how this was phrased in Nazi jargon with its unspeakable contempt for humankind; nowadays, one would say "ethnic cleansing," though that does not sound much better. The man in charge was, characteristically, *Reichsführer* SS Heinrich Himmler, whom Hitler also appointed "Reich-Commissar for the Strengthening of German people and folklore" in October 1939. Besides South Tyrol, he was then additionally responsible for resettlement and Germanization efforts in the occupied territories of eastern and southeastern Europe.

How were the events of 23 June possible? Who were the initiators, and who were those chiefly to blame? Were they on the German side and/or among the Italians? These are questions that also assumed central importance after 1945 in connection with the demand for self-determination, to say nothing of the moral aspects of the problem. Even if for some people — depending on which side they take — the question of attributing guilt has always been cut and dried, this matter is just not that simple. There were those on both the German and Italian sides who saw resettlement of the South Tyroleans as the solution to the problem, and held this view long before 1939.

Exchange and resettlement of entire ethnic groups in order to solve minority problems and to create borders between states and nationalities in agreement with these circumstances was, in and of itself, nothing new. This was the result of the nineteenth-century principle of the national state taken to its ultimate conclusion and thought through to its final ramifications — an approach that Greece and Turkey had practiced in grand style in the early 1920s, and which, in turn, enflamed the imaginations of many a nationalist elsewhere. With respect to South Tyrol, the name Tolomei comes up here as well; he and his comrade-in-arms Adriano Colocci-Vespucci were maintaining as early as 1914 that the right of the nation had precedence over the right of domicile, and it was from this principle that they derived Italy's right

> to resettle the German contaminants that dominate the region of Alto Adige today to the almost complete exclusion of others, and to kick them back beyond the Brenner where they belong. . . . The 200,000 Germans who are polluting South Tyrol must shoulder the biblical blame for the sins of their fathers.[12]

The Option of 1939 finally led Tolomei to believe in the eventual consummation of his life's work. He welcomed the resettlement agreement and interpreted it as an "eternal guarantee" of the Brenner border as the boundary of the Italian state and nation, which he said was exactly what Hitler had promised him during their talks in Munich in 1928. Tolomei took a lion's share of the credit in bringing about the Option.

On the other side were men like Wilhelm Rohmeder and Michael Mayr, proponents of the Tyrolean People's League that had been founded in 1905. For them, the people of Trentino were Italianized Rhaetians or Germans, and the solution would be the Germanicizing of Italian names; they regarded the southern slope of the Alps as the natural boundary. A list of new, artificial Germand names for the original Italian names already exited: Gartensee for Lake Garda, Reif for the city of Riva, and so forth. It is certainly not surprising that when Mayr served as Austrian chancellor in 1921, he could hardly lend his support to the autonomy rights of the South Tyroleans.

Coming up with plans and bizarre ideas is one thing; turning them into practical policy is quite another. With Mussolini in power, Tolomei's Italianization program was being implemented, but it was not until Hitler assumed power that resettlement became feasible. The Austrian historian Karl Stuhlpfarrer gave a very accurate description of the connection between Nazi policies and South Tyrol:

> Foreign policy objectives, alliance considerations, the ideology of national character and customs, and *Lebensraum* dogma constituted the logic of National Socialist policymaking, which, with the inevitability that was inherent in this system, steered a certain course toward the resettlement of the South Tyroleans.[13]

Following the Anschluß of Austria, talk of resettlement was in the air. And as with the Anschluß itself, Hermann Göring seems to have initially been the driving force here as well. Göring had maintained his Italian connection since the failed Beer Hall *Putsch* of 1923; he was familiar with the South Tyrol problem, and, above all, he knew how important this issue was to the Italian Fascists. Thus, it should come as no surprise that he first spoke in concrete terms about a solution to the problem through resettlement in January 1937 in Rome with German Ambassador Ulrich von Hassell: the ethnic Germans of South Tyrol would have to be sacrificed to the alliance with Italy. The first preparatory talks between Italians and Germans took place in March/April 1938, whereby it is interesting to note that it was not Foreign Minister Joachim von Ribbentrop or Himmler but rather Göring was the central figure on the German side (along with the representatives of the Foreign Ministry: State Secretary Ernst von Weizsaecker and the top officers in the Italian Section, General Consul Max Lorenz and Envoy Kurt Heinburg). The Italian participants in these talks were Foreign Minister Galeazzo Ciano, Mussolini's son-in-law; racial theorist Giovanni Preziosi; and their top diplomats in Berlin, Ambassador Bernardo Attolico, Embassy Counsellor Massimo Magistrati, and General Consul Giuseppe Renzetti — all advocates of a "radical solution." Ciano noted in his diary that it would have to be intimated to the Germans that it would be opportune to reabsorb their people because Alto Adige was geographically an Italian land. Because one cannot move mountains and reroute rivers, they would simply have to transfer the people.

Both sides were fundamentally in agreement that the South Tyrol question could be solved once and for all through resettlement, which is precisely why these exploratory talks took on such tremendous significance for the subsequent course of events. The immediate result came in March with a memorandum written by General Consul Max Lorenz, the gist of which would become and remain the basis of later German policy: total resettlement of the South Tyroleans to an area that would be made available in the future by conquest in the East.

There was not a similarly clear conception from the very start on the Italian side, which explains some of the puzzling events that transpired in the fall of 1939. Only a few opinion leaders — including, however, the influential Chief of Police Arturo Bocchini — favored such a radical solution, even if they argued for it at the start for tactical reasons, as in the case of Ciano, for example, or Mastromattei (whose stance was, indeed, not at all clear). Most wanted only a partial resettlement: anything resembling a fifth column ought to disappear, along with approximately 10,000 Germans and ex-Austrians; 20,000-40,000 undesirables, especially "dangerous" South Tyroleans, intellectuals, and the like; and the unemployed as well as blue- and white-collar workers, who could easily be replaced by Italians anyway. Italy would be able to handle the remainder. There was absolutely no sentiment for resettlement of peasant farmers from mountainous regions, and certainly no one anticipated that the South Tyroleans would overwhelmingly decide in favor of Germany. After all, in early 1939 even Otto Bene, the German general consul in Milan who was also responsible for South Tyrol, estimated the number of those wishing to resettle at 1,000-2,000 at the very most.

After Hitler's visit to Italy in May 1938, inflamed feelings cooled off initially, but Rome's mistrust of Hitler's guarantee of the Brenner border had not totally dissipated. After all, he had declared in connection with the Czechoslovakia crisis, "We don't want any Czechs at all!" and then followed that statement up in March 1939 by "crushing the Czech rump," and did so without consulting Mussolini. Without this obvious violation of these "boundaries as dictated by ethnic policy," that inhuman agreement of June 1939 would most probably never have come into existence, but now the Fascists wanted to play it safe and take the Germans at their word, especially since they had good cards in their hand in the ongoing negotiations to reach a "Pact of Steel." Embassy Counsellor Magistrati addressed this issue on 5 April 1939 in the Foreign Ministry and proposed total resettlement as the answer to the South Tyrol question. The fact that tangible economic interests also played a role in this entire undertaking from the very start was clear. Italy wanted to redeem the resettlement assets with foreign exchange that had been frozen in Austria since the Anschluß, whereas, conversely, the German Reich, which was suffering under a catastrophic shortage of foreign reserves, wanted to use the redemption of the assets primarily to finance the import of raw materials from Italy and to pay the wages of approximately 60,000 Italian guest workers in the Reich.

This point would later be the cause of tremendous difficulties. A special exchange rate was ultimately established for the Reichsmark and the Lira (1 RM = 4.5 Lire, as compared to the official rate of 1 RM = 7.63 Lire). Indeed, during the talks held in October, Italy limited the total sum to 1 billion Lire, which was, according to South Tyrolean historian Leopold Steurer, only 1/15 to 1/20 of the estimated total assets of the German-speaking South Tyroleans. At first glance, the conclusion that Steurer draws from this is convincing, namely: "By means of these economic provisions, Italy provided itself with assurance that the number of those who would actually emigrate would not reach or would hardly surpass the maximum number it desired." In other words, it would never come to total resettlement — an interpretation that goes too far. As far as the economic aspects of the Option are concerned, it is clear that Italy did not wish to use this roundabout method to purchase a province that it had received free of charge in 1919. It is also quite correct that from 1940 on, the Italians and South Tyroleans used the valuation issue as an instrument to delay resettlement, though it would have ultimately been impossible to prevent it in this way. What did indeed prevent it was — from the Nazi point of view — the unfortunate outcome of the war! One can well proceed under the assumption that if the war had turned out differently, Himmler would have carried out the resettlement program and probably used the very same methods he had already employed in eastern and southeastern

Europe with ruthless disregard for any sort of special Reichsmark-Lira exchange rate, financial limitations, or transport problems, and the South Tyrolean farmers would have become a "German peasant bulwark" somewhere in the East.

Things had not yet reached that point, but Himmler had decided by the end of May 1939 at the very latest to go ahead with total resettlement. On 16 June Hitler officially made him responsible for the overall planning of the operation. For Himmler, this must have been a fascinating assignment; everything that followed bore his personal touch. A gigantic bureaucracy was organized, as South Tyrol became the first field test of Nazi "human resource deployment."

The Position of the *Völkischer Kampfring Südtirols* (VKS)

Up to 23 June 1939, the subject of the Option and resettlement was primarily a German-Italian affair; thereafter, it was a matter for the South Tyroleans, and, first and foremost, a concern of the VKS. This is undoubtedly the most sorrowful chapter of this story, one that has left an indelible trace upon the history of South Tyrol. Here, the responsibility of the VKS is beyond question, as is the fact that its ranks were rife with committed Nazis for whom there can be no exculpation.

We know from Leopold Steurer that in April 1939 a VKS delegation travelled to Munich where *Reichsleiter* Martin Bormann and SS-*Oberführer* Hermann Behrends informed them "officially" that Hitler had decided the South Tyrol question "in favor of resettlement." The VKS initially rejected resettlement. A memorandum on this issue stated that this was the only "order from Hitler" that would not be obeyed; otherwise, they would remain "true to all the commitments we have so often reiterated in the past: we will tenaciously defend our homeland and our people; in all other respects, we will subordinate ourselves in loyalty, trust and obedience to the *Führer*." In another passage, it was said to be

> incomprehensible that such a plan could even be considered in light of the fact that the concept of the indivisible unity of blood and soil is among the guiding principles of the National Socialist *Weltanschauung*. In the Reich as well, one ought not

lose sight of the danger inherent in establishing a precedent that could one day have disastrous ethnic policy consequences for the Reich itself. . . . A people that for more than a thousand years has been a bulwark of Germany in the south and has done its duty at the forefront of every battle for the German *Lebensraum*, many of whose farmers work land that has been passed down from generation to generation in the same family for centuries will never willingly allow itself to be resettled. . . . Voluntarily renouncing a piece of the German *Lebensraum*, though, cannot be the solution, and is unworthy of a revived Reich.

For the VKS, the conclusion to be drawn was obvious: "Thus, it must be clear that we absolutely reject any thought of resettlement."[14] That at least sounded like refusal to obey an order. When the Berlin Agreement was then announced, the first reaction of the VKS was likewise rejection. At a joint meeting with representatives of the German Association, it was decided that emigration was out of the question.

But only a few days later, the VKS did a complete about-face. Suddenly, their position was:

The German people of South Tyrol will leave its old homeland and head off to a new one in the Greater German Reich to rescue and carry on our national customs and traditions, to live up to the ideals of our forefathers, and to fulfill the obligation to instill our people's values in our children. It has not been in vain that the South Tyrolean people has lived twenty years long among strangers, and we know that, following resettlement, German life on the banks of the Eisack and the Etsch will be no more.[15]

In Leopold Steurer's opinion, the VKS's "*Nibelungen* loyalty and ancient Germanic oaths of fealty which bound a band of young nobles to a peer leader" were responsible for this shift. He expressly rejects citing the "Sicilian legend" — the rumor that the Italians would deport all those who did not opt for Germany to Sicily, Abyssinia, or other regions, but, in any case, "south of the Po" — as a factor that played a role in the VKS altering its stance.

We know from numerous contemporary eyewitness reports, which have also been confirmed by an oral history project, that this rumor was the decisive factor that influenced very many, if not most, South Tyroleans in reaching their decision to go. Lothar von Sternbach, himself a "stayer," conceded, "The threat of forced resettlement to the south made more people into 'goers' than the Nazi propaganda." This legend was a tactical masterpiece carried out by Berlin. When "Nibelungen loyalty" did not suffice, a little extra help had to be provided. General Consul Otto Bene took on this role. On 29 June, he officially informed the German expatriates in Meran about Berlin's decision. On this occasion, he was the first to speak of a possible deportation to the south of all those South Tyroleans who did not opt for Germany. Immediately thereafter, the VKS made its decision. Bene did a terrific job of concealing the origin of this rumor; actually, it was later attributed almost exclusively to Mastromattei, who first made reference to this on 6 July and who likewise immediately recognized it as an extremely useful instrument to increase the readiness of the South Tyroleans to accept resettlement.

The Italians were struck completely blind during those weeks. They continued with their policy of threats and harassment oblivious to the fact that they were about to trigger a landslide. In July, the government was already ordering the dismissal of all Germans in the civil service and all female personnel employed in the hospitality industry, who had to be replaced by men from Lombardy, Liguria, and Piedmont. All tourists had to leave South Tyrol. The owners of tobacco shops and newspaper stands were no longer permitted to speak German with their customers.

When the Italians finally realized what was looming — the distinct possibility that what would remain behind would be a depopulated region for which they were going to pay a fortune (which they had gotten free after World War I) and which could never be revived and made to flourish like it had before — it was already too late. No matter how many times Mastromattei promised that, of course, no one was going to be deported to the south, his denials had precisely the opposite effect. This man's credibility in the eyes of the South Tyroleans was so low that no one believed a single thing he said any more. Perhaps if Mussolini had come forth with a few clarifying words, it would have been possible to turn things around — at least that is what the "stayers" hoped and, for this very reason, sent a delegation to Rome in November. But Himmler triumphed. The intervention of his personal adjutant Karl Wolff succeeded in convincing Mussolini to refuse to receive the delegation — a momentous decision that now left the "stayers" standing there with empty hands. Then on 17 November, SS-*Gruppenführer* Karl Wolff signed a particularly perfidious agreement with Police Chief Bocchini and Guido Buffarini-Guidi, the state secretary in the Ministry of the Interior: It was unmistakably clear that the resettlement was a final and complete ethnic solution after which there would no longer be an ethnic minority issue in Alto Adige.

To Go or to Stay? Disunity among the South Tyroleans

By this point, a gigantic wave of propaganda was already rolling across the land. Now that the VKS leaders had made up their minds, their job was to be able to report to the *Führer* a result that was befitting National Socialism, and they had until 31 December 1939 to do so. Some of them undoubtedly hoped that if they would be able to deliver such a "profession of loyalty," then the *Führer* might bring not only his South Tyrolean people but their land as well "home into the Reich." Thoughts turned to the Saarland, which explains why VKS leader Peter Hofer reported to Berlin in early January 1940 an Option vote result that had been "rounded up" slightly to 90.7 percent (from approximately 86 percent), precisely how the 1935 vote in the Saarland had turned out. The hope was deceptive, and Himmler's response sobering: the *Führer* was "pleased" by the people's decision; he was said to have reviewed the vote count and "taken note" of it. Then Himmler offered praise, "Germany is proud of its South Tyrolean people." But in the same breath, he destroyed all hope of being able to remain in that land: "I repeat that the South Tyrolean people will be resettled as a single unified group, and that its leaders will have the opportunity to familiarize themselves with the regions that will come into consideration for resettlement before a final decision on the selection of the land is made."[16] The assurance of a unified, contiguous area of settlement was a trump card that the VKS had successfully played in its propaganda. The people believed it, and they did not seem to be disturbed by the fact that this region would first have to be taken by the *Wehrmacht* and its inhabitants driven out. There was agreement that it would have to be a beautiful region, at least as beautiful as South Tyrol, even more beautiful if possible, and with enough land that even fourth sons would someday have farms of their own. Many realized only too late that this land of milk and honey did not exist. The Beskides in Galicia, the first area that Himmler proposed, was not quite right. Some South Tyroleans were acquainted with this region from their service during World War I, and this would have been a tough sale, so this plan immediately sank back into oblivion. The propagandists simply stuck by their claim that everything would be exactly the way it was in South Tyrol and that everyone would remain together.

The threat of forced resettlement in the south and the assurance of a unified, contiguous area of settlement were the chief weapons in the VKS's propaganda war between "goers" and "stayers." Where their propaganda was ineffective, the Nazis resorted to terror. The most terrible chapter in the history of South Tyrol would now be written by the South Tyroleans themselves! This is the very reason why the deep wounds that were inflicted in those days were so difficult to heal and ruptured over and over again.

"German or Dago! Stand by one another and build a new homeland together!" These were catchy and successful slogans, and this propaganda was hard to resist even by those who had maintained a rather indifferent attitude toward politics up to that point. The flood of fliers, inflammatory broadsides, and chain letters inundated even the most remote mountain village, with the chief aim of denouncing and ostracizing those planning to stay. "Handbills in honor of the traitors to the German people" gave a good working over to every single stayer in a village, not even stopping short of invading a person's private sphere. They were the "Wops," the true "traitors." There was talk of Gypsies and Jews, and of the fear of having to work and serve in the army during wartime in the Third Reich. The biographies of those wishing to stay were examined in order to find "weaknesses," and this material was funneled into the political debates. Threats and violence were the order of the day. On the façade of a stayer's inn in which a Jewish fruit dealer had spent the night, "Hotel Israel" was painted; another was smeared with liquid manure; some barns went up in flames; stayers' children were pelted with stones, window panes were smashed, and houses were smeared with feces and dirt. Friendships, neighborhoods, and families were ripped apart. One of the most popular "stayers" and after World War II one of the most influential politicians, Friedl Volgger, describes it in his memoirs in these terms, "What the Jews were in the Third Reich is what some of the South Tyroleans became in the eyes of their fanatical countrymen."

In practically every village, meetings were held of those who wanted to stay and those planning to go. Thousands of fliers, defamatory pamphlets, satirical poems, and chain letters were circulating among the population of South Tyrol.

A great many South Tyroleans simply could not cope with this kind of propaganda that poured down upon them. After going through tremendous mental anguish, they opted with a heavy heart for what was in their view the lesser of two evils: German citizenship and resettlement. In their heart of hearts, no doubt, they still hoped for liberation after the "final victory." The reasoning that Archbishop Celestino Endrici of Trient set down in May 1940 in a memorandum to the Vatican has to this day lost none of its validity:

> None of these arguments [employed by the Nazi propaganda] would have had any success among 80 percent of the population if the entire Option had not afforded the opportunity to unleash a reaction against the government's methods as suggested by Senator Tolomei and carried out by Prefect Mastromattei — methods that are today regarded as idiotic even by the Italian authorities themselves. Only these circumstances can explain the severity of the fervor that gripped the majority of the population and led even simple peasant farmers to heed outside agitators, to close their ears to their own parish priests, and to give up homesteads that had been in their family for centuries and of which they would previously have been unwilling to part with even a single square meter.[17]

The stayers were for a clear rejection of the brutal solution of resettlement and were prepared to accept the consequences. At that point, they seemed to be fighting a losing battle and no doubt secretly hoped that their fate would somehow take a turn for the better, but they stood up and suffered for their convictions, first among their own countrymen and then under the Nazis, in a struggle that sometimes led all the way to Dachau concentration camp — as happened to Friedl Volgger.

After the Option in 1939, almost 75,000 South Tyroleans leave their homeland in the following years — a drain that proves to be a severe burden for the land after 1945, when only about 20,000 return. The picture shows a train leaving Bozen main station in May 1940.

When one reads today how the VKS leaders described things in those days, one gets an impression of where political fanaticism can lead. On 11 November Peter Hofer wrote the following words to General Consul Otto Bene:

> When I consider that this South Tyrolean mountain folk has been for centuries instilled with the alien slogan of the old *"für Gott, Kaiser und Vaterland"* [for God, Emperor and Fatherland] and until recently did not even know what Germany was, then we all must acknowledge in profound gratitude this conscious process of becoming a unified people that would sooner give up its 1000-year-old homeland in a German landscape of unsurpassed beauty than to become separated from its German culture and traditions. And for this result, which, in its simplicity and its overwhelming dimensions that every German can look upon with pride, is so utterly moving to us at the end

of this fateful year, we want, above all, to express our thanks to the *Führer*.[18]

Karl Nicolussi in a letter dated 10 November to Peter Hofer, spoke of a positive "referendum psychosis" of "model villages" in which the community decided to submit a "report of unanimity." The vote had turned into a "people's rally"; the South Tyroleans were said to be "in a joyful mood" and "for example, in Gossensass could not even be held back by the parish priest who confronted the procession of voters on the road between Gossensass and Sterzing." Nicolussi ended his letter with the following sentences:

> I was never so proud of our people as I have been these last two days, during which I have had the opportunity to admire its supreme national values. After years of countless disappointments . . . an entire people has decided to leave all of its belongings and, above all, its homeland without any certain knowledge about its future, filled only with belief and trust in Germany and the *Führer*. By God, the *Führer* has never seen such Germans. But outsiders will never be able to grasp what our movement has done to bring this about.[19]

The Catholic Church

The Catholic Church and the Option is a very special topic. South Tyrol, with an almost 100 percent Catholic population, suffered deep wounds that have never fully healed. The name of the Brixen Prince-Bishop Johannes Geisler will no doubt forever remain associated with this issue. Geisler was originally from North Tyrol; he was a kind, charming, and quite humane person, but also a very weak prince of the Church who failed at the decisive moment. He initially vacillated between giving his blessings to resettlement and rejecting it, but he then revised his position as he came more and more under the influence of his General Vicar Alois Pompanin. Pompanin was a Ladin, a fanatical advocate of resettlement into the Reich, and an ardent admirer of Hitler.

The Pope's admonishments to proceed with caution in this question went unheeded. As a result, there soon developed a rift between the bishop and his clergy, who in late October 1939 were forbidden to conduct any further propagandizing. The clergy was opposed to the Option for the Third Reich; they called attention to the persecution of the Church and the program of euthanasia in Germany, and were subjected to censorship by their bishop on this point. When Bishop Endrici came out against resettlement in the newsletter he published for the German communicants of his diocese (which was by far the largest portion of South Tyrol, including the Eisack Valley up to the first hamlet south of Brixen, and in Vinschgau extended all the way to the parish of Prad am Stilfserjoch), Bishop Geisler did not co-sign.

The Brixen cathedral chapter was also arrayed against Geisler. The confrontation with him went so far that it even submitted a request to Rome that the bishop be replaced. Although that did not occur, the communiqué from the Vatican Counsellor Giuseppe Misuraca that Geisler was free to resign and leave the diocese if he wished was not exactly a vote of confidence in the bishop.

On 25 June 1940 (for the Church, the Option deadline had been extended to 30 June 1940), Geisler opted for Germany with the argument, "The good shepherd follows his flock." It had apparently never occurred to him that a good shepherd provides direction to his flock. Geisler's decision was exactly what the Nazis had been waiting for. They exploited it accordingly for propaganda purposes, although it was, of course, too late to have had an influence on the Option result. The majority of the clergy, on the other hand, were for remaining in their homeland; only about 20 percent decided to follow the bishop, and among the Germans of the Diocese of Trient, the figure was only about 10 percent.

Did the Catholic Church thus fail its faithful in their hour of need? The Catholic Church does not consist solely of bishops and general vicars. With the votes they cast, the majority of the pastors gave clear expression to their opposition to the Nazi regime, although their attitude was based above all on religious grounds. Indeed, the way in which the conflict between the bishop and the clergy was conducted was most peculiar and extremely un-Christian. Equally remarkable was the way those involved went back to business as usual after 1945 as if nothing at all had happened.

V. 1940-1945: Resettlement and "Reunification"

Resettlement

By September 1939, the *Amtliche deutsche Ein- und Rückwandererstelle* (ADERST, or Official German Immigration and Remigration Bureau) had been set up with its headquarters in Bozen and branch offices in all cities and larger villages in South Tyrol. Although this group had been established "solely" to deal with Option issues and to organize and carry out immigration to Germany, it soon developed into a kind of German parallel administration, which the Fascists were grudgingly forced to accept. The ADERST under the leadership of Wilhelm Luig as well as the *Arbeitsgemeinschaft der Optanten* (ADO, or Working Group for Those Opting for Germany) that had come into being in January 1940 as an outgrowth of the VKS and was headed by Peter Hofer were now the chief contacts for emigrants. These people could once again be openly "German"; the German school was permitted to resume activities, as were German associations. Beginning in the spring of 1940, there were "German language courses" set up to augment the Italian elementary schools, with instruction offered in the afternoon. The course content was strongly influenced by National Socialist thinking, and the teaching materials came from the Third Reich; after all, the chief aim of this undertaking was not to provide language instruction to the children of those who had opted for Germany, but rather to properly socialize future "national comrades." In the fall of 1940, so-called "Schools for Ethnic Germans" were set up in Rufach in Alsace (for boys) and in Achern in Baden (for girls), though they more closely resembled indoctrination institutes than normal prep schools. Whoever attended one of them was marked for life by the experience.

Several former VKS members were being prepared to assume leadership positions in the new settlement area. A select group of deserving South Tyrolean "comrades" finally received special political training at SS bases throughout the Third Reich (and particularly at the Sonthofen facility in Allgaeu).

In South Tyrol itself, the traditions that Fascism had repressed for twenty years — folk dancing, oompah-band music, marching societies, the cultivation of folk singing and native costumes — were now smoothly integrated into the National Socialist *Weltanschauung*. During this time, the stayers — those South Tyroleans who had either not voted or had decided to retain Italian citizenship — continued to be scorned by their countrymen, and remained outsiders in South Tyrolean society. They were subjected to all sorts of harassment, and their children were excluded from German language instruction. When Italy entered the war on 10 June 1940, both sides rejoiced: those who were remaining because they were convinced that Germany with Italy as its ally would lose the war and the South Tyroleans would be able to remain on their land and those who had opted for Germany because at least now the stayers would have to do military service, too (and in the Italian Army, no less). But the stayers quickly found a solution to this problem as well, and did so, interestingly enough, in cooperation with local Fascist leaders. Heads of farming operations, owners and lessees alike, were exempt from the draft. Hundreds of lease agreements were concluded, whereby the Italians knew perfectly well that some were mere shams. Once an enlistment order arrived, a lease agreement was presented to the appropriate official, and it was accepted. The Italian state also showed a number of other considerations to the South Tyroleans who remained: there was tax relief for families with many children and for farmers in mountainous regions, and it was once again permitted to acquire property. On 21 March 1940, Mussolini received their delegation and assured them that those who had opted for Italy would be allowed to remain in their homeland and that "no one had ever considered transplanting them to other parts of the empire."

The actual resettlement is a story in and of itself. Germany and Italy were pursuing fundamentally different interests. Germany wanted to augment its workforce, to recruit volunteers and draft-age men, to settle peasants in conquered territories as a bulwark of Germanic culture, and to receive the compensation for the South Tyrolean assets with which to offset Italian payment demands on the Third Reich. Italy, on the other hand, wanted to get rid of the German-speaking inhabitants in the wake of the failure of its assimilation policy in South Tyrol, and to thereby eliminate a seat of unrest on its northern border.

The issue of paramount importance was the emigration of the political and social elite: entrepreneurs, self-employed professionals, and farmers with large-scale orchards and vineyards. Peasant farmers from mountainous regions could just as well stay, since they could hardly be replaced by Italians. The VKS wanted to maintain the core of the South Tyrolean population, the peasantry, the province's economic substance, and the people's cultural heritage in order to be able to recreate similar structures and to assume political leadership in the new, contiguous territory of resettlement. The first of these emigrants were convicts who had opted for Germany and were now transferred there; in addition, there were soldiers who had been serving in the Italian Army and had been immediately discharged once they had opted for Germany, as well as self-employed individuals who had been deprived of their livelihood, for example, due to their business license having been revoked.

Beginning in mid-November 1939, a great many resettlement transports began arriving in Innsbruck. In a memorandum dated 12 December 1939, SS-*Gruppenführer* Karl Wolff indicated that 4,092 South Tyroleans had been resettled up through 9 December 1939; by year's end, the figure was approximately 11,500.

In January 1940, Mussolini was assured that, on average, 200 to 250 South Tyroleans were emigrating each day. It was taken for granted that the final decision on the contiguous area of settlement would soon be made. Until then, those who did not own property, wage-dependent laborers, civil servants, political persecutees, and those who had become economically unviable — in short, the "dispensable" segment of the South Tyrolean population — were to be resettled. However, no damage was to be inflicted on the South Tyrolean economy by emigration; therefore, a three-stage resettlement plan was proposed:

1. *Reichsdeutsche*: Germans and Austrians who had taken up residence in South Tyrol;
2. *Volksdeutsche*: ethnic Germans whose existence was not *bodengebunden* (tied to the soil);
3. *bodengebundene Volksdeutsche*.

Due to the composition of this first wave of emigration, the local population suffered its severest diminishment among those employed in industry, in the crafts and trades, in the transportation sector, and in domestic service. Agriculture suffered the least. The fact that only 9 percent of those who resettled came from agriculture led to the post-1945 claim and myth of the farmer as "the savior of the land." The farmers who left the province were settled onto farms either in Tyrol and Vorarlberg or in so-called "repatriated" or "liberated" territories that had been taken by force of arms and incorporated into the German Reich, such as Luxemburg and Alsace.

About 50 percent of those approximately 75,000 *Optanten* who actually left South Tyrol emigrated in 1940; thereafter, resettlement began to flag: in 1941, 24 percent; in 1942, 8 percent; in 1943, a mere 4 percent. There were a number of reasons for this. One of the most important was certainly the fact that the final selection of a resettlement territory had not been made with the mandatory approval of the ADO leadership. In the spring of 1940, rumors of a possible resettlement to Alsace-Lorraine surfaced; in June 1940, following the conclusion of the military campaign in France, Himmler decided upon Burgundy as the new resettlement territory. There, the new South Tyrol would be built and the Burgundian cities would simply be renamed Bozen, Meran, Brixen, Bruneck, and so forth. The ADO leaders undertook an inspection tour of Burgundy at that time; one of the few pieces of historical evidence documenting this trip is a photo depicting, among others, Karl Tinzl.

Hitler had other ideas, since his ceasefire with France called for the establishment of the Vichy government whose jurisdiction included Burgundy. Then, the Crimean Peninsula in the Black Sea was mentioned as a place to resettle the South Tyroleans.

The absence of a territory, however, was not the only reason for the delay in resettlement. Other factors also came into play. The initial enthusiasm quickly gave way to disillusionment. The first ones to actually go through with resettlement had been received by none other than Nazi-*Gauleiter* Franz Hofer at the train depot in Innsbruck, the obligatory first way station on this journey, with banners proclaiming "South Tyroleans, the *Führer* has been expecting you," or "South Tyroleans, Greater Germany welcomes you," with rousing march music and fiery speeches. But all that changed very quickly, and even before the end of 1940 there was no longer any time to spare for such displays. To this can be added the difficulties in securing lodging and furnishing apartments for the emigrants. There was no longer much mention of the grand promises that had been made in the past. The emigrants were housed in emergency quarters (sublet rooms, barracks, monasteries, army bases) and had to accept jobs that often were not quite what they were used to.

Furthermore, there were tremendous difficulties and delays with the appraisal of and final payment for the South Tyrolean assets of those who had opted for Germany; for this reason, many delayed their departure for as long as it took to finally establish the value of their assets. By the end of 1942, only 9,700 of 63,000 applicants had received their final appraisal. By August 1942, Himmler was urging the responsible authorities in Bozen to speed up emigration, and to cease accepting the excuse that individuals were waiting for the final selection of a contiguous resettlement territory. Moreover, following the dismissal of General Consul Otto Bene, the top man in the German resettlement agency in Bozen since October 1941 was Ludwig Mayr-Falkenberg. He was anything but a dutiful civil servant who strictly toed the party line, and he did everything possible to delay resettlement.

Nazi *Gauleiter* Franz Hofer

With the overthrow of Mussolini, Italy's switch to the side of the Allies and the occupation of South Tyrol and northern Italy by German troops on 9 September 1943, the overwhelming majority of the South Tyroleans felt themselves to have been freed from the Italian yoke. The symbol of that yoke, Tolomei, was arrested by the Germans and sent via Innsbruck and Dachau concentration camp to Thüringen in Germany where he was interned until the end of the war. After twenty years of Fascist rule, the long-awaited day of liberation seemed to have arrived. Nevertheless, the hoped-for official annexation of South Tyrol to the German Reich and thus the reunification of Tyrol did not materialize. A sort of *de facto* annexation did take place; but from the perspective of constitutional law, South Tyrol remained a part of Italy. It was part of Mussolini's new (pseudo-) *Repubblica Sociale di Salò,* the existence of which depended on the grace of Berlin. The subsequent twenty months of

German civil administration are nevertheless interesting in a number of respects, in that certain preconditions were established that would turn out to be decisive for the immediate postwar period.

Hitler's order, dated 10 September 1943, set up two operations zones in Italy, which was now occupied by German troops: the "Adriatic coastal region" and the "Alpine foothills (*Alpenvorland*) region." The latter consisted of the provinces of Trient, Bozen, and Belluno. The civil administration set up for these areas meant that they were separate from the rest of Italy. In these operations zones, the military commanders were assigned civilian advisors called "supreme commissioners." For the *Alpenvorland*, this was *Gauleiter* Franz Hofer, and over the next two years he would play a key role in the decisions made there. Hofer pursued policies aimed at bringing about a *de facto* amalgamation of his operations zone with the Tyrol-Vorarlberg *Gau* (administrative district). He wanted at the very least to merge South Tyrol into his *Gau* — in other words, to bring about the reunification of Tyrol. Right from the start, he urged Hitler and top government officials to annex this region.

Nevertheless, he failed to accomplish this. Hitler showed consideration for Mussolini, who had been freed by German paratroopers on 12 September 1943; he did not want to show up his ally. The Reich government therefore forbade all measures that could give the impression of an official annexation. South Tyrol thus officially remained a part of the Republic of Salò, even though that government's influence there was practically nil.

An order dated 6 November 1943 mandated universal conscription throughout the entire operations zone. Whoever sought to avoid enlistment could expect to receive the death penalty; relatives of anyone who fled to escape service could be taken hostage. In South Tyrol, 2,000-man police regiments ("Bozen," "Brixen," "Schlanders," "Alpenvorland") were raised. In the process of conscription, there was in principle no differentiation between those who had opted for Germany and those who had chosen to stay; in fact, the stayers were the first to be sent to the front. This meant that members of both groups were assigned to German units, a clear contravention of international law, but this was just another matter to which no one paid any attention at the time. Young men were even forced to join units of the *Waffen*-SS. The police regiments, which were placed under the command of SS-*Gruppenführer* Karl Wolff and later renamed SS-*Polizei*, were deployed in South Tyrol, in Trentino and in the Province of Udine to provide security at key installations and to conduct anti-partisan operations. When the police regiment "Brixen" refused to take a loyalty oath, it was punished by being transferred to Silesia. Those South Tyroleans who remained in the province served in the *Wehrmacht*, the police and the *Südtiroler Ordnungsdienst* (SOD, or South Tyrolean Guard). The SOD was belatedly recognized by the German command and armed with captured Italian weapons. The build-up proceeded very rapidly; by October, it was already 9,000 men strong. From the very beginning, though, there developed a competitive struggle for the supreme command of the SOD, with the *Wehrmacht*, the police, and Hofer all pursuing their own interests. Hofer eventually had his way, and the SOD was placed under his command. The SOD was assigned patrol and watch duties, as well as being used in anti-partisan operations. For example, in June 1944 elements of the SOD were involved in the murder of leading Trentino resistance fighters and the arrest of the province's most famous partisan, Gianantonio Manci.

The 11th Company of the police regiment "Bozen," once it had completed its training, had been transferred to Rome. The capital was then declared an open city, and most of the German troops stationed there were withdrawn. On 23 March 1944 in the Via Rasella, this company was the target of a bomb attack carried out by Communist partisans that claimed the lives of thirty-three South Tyroleans.

In reprisal, SS men under the command of Colonel Herbert Kappler murdered 335 Italian hostages in the Ardeatine caves. The victims of the *fosse ardeatine* were between fourteen and seventy-five years of age. After Kappler's SS men had carried out the massacre, the entrances to the caves were blown up with high explosives. According to the practice in effect at the time, these reprisal executions should have been carried out by the unit that had been the target of the original attack — that is, the Bozen company — but its commander declined on the grounds that his men were Catholic and somewhat older individuals who could not bring themselves to shoot defenseless hostages. In the 1990s, these reprisal executions were the subject of an investigation by the Italian judiciary.

Even if Italian territorial sovereignty and its national borders remained formally inviolable and the Lira was still legal tender in the operations zone, the German authorities had, practically speaking, assumed power and saw to it that there were corresponding concessions made to the South Tyroleans. As early as September 1943, Hofer decreed that the German and Italian languages would have equal status. From then on, German could once again legally be spoken in public everywhere, and both languages were on an equal footing for the conduct of official government business. German and Ladin place names were also reintroduced and publicly displayed alongside the Italian place names. It was undoubtedly out of consideration for the Republic of Salò that the Italian names were maintained. The *Podestà* were replaced by local mayors, and the children of stayers could now attend the German school, which was converted to a "normal" institution of learning offering instruction in all the usual subjects.

The German authorities now proceeded with deliberate measures aimed at the press. The *Athesia* publishing house was closed; the *Dolomiten* (that had been put out by Athesia and had published editorials critical of the Nazis up until 1943), the Fascist *Alpenzeitung*, and the Italian-language *Provincia di Bolzano* had to cease publication. The only daily that was then still in print was the newly-founded *Bozner Tagblatt*. The Italians in South Tyrol now no longer had a daily newspaper of their own; all that remained for them was *Il Trentino*; newspapers from the Republic of Salò were forbidden to be imported into the Alpenvorland operations zone. Radio broadcasts were in German only. The ban on the activities of all political parties had an even more severe impact on them: the Fascist Party was outlawed, just as the NSDAP was. For the Italians, this meant the collapse of any and all infrastructure contributing to public life in South Tyrol. The immigrant Italians had by no means established roots in the area. Nothing had grown up naturally; rather, the Fascists had quickly set up everything in just a few years — from local bars to soccer clubs. Nevertheless, there was no emigration; on the contrary, there was actually immigration of Italians to South Tyrol. The reason for this was simple: the Italians in South Tyrol were not called up for military service. In order to prevent this influx, Gauleiter Franz Hofer enacted strict laws regulating immigration to and temporary residency in the operations zone. To enforce these provisions, a checkpoint was set up in the vicinity of Borghetto on the old southern border of Tyrol.

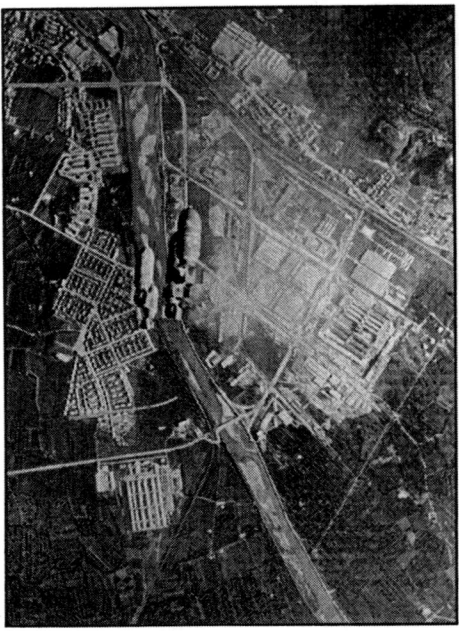

The railroad between Innsbruck and Bozen is a vital supply-line for the German troops in Italy. Bombs are falling on Bozen. On the left is the *semirurali*, on the right the industrial zone.

German rule set the Nazi machinery of annihilation in motion in Italy as well. This affected the Jews above all. Up to 1943, they had been able to live — though not exactly flourish — in Fascist Italy. Nevertheless, they could survive. That changed immediately once German troops moved in. The sole organized Jewish community in the operations zone was in Meran, where there were sixty members at the time the Germans arrived, the others having previously moved away. As early as 16 September 24 of them were arrested by the SOD under the leadership of the Gestapo, and sent to the Reichenau camp near Innsbruck. Of this group, nineteen were murdered in Auschwitz, four died in Reichenau, and one woman survived. The handful of Jews in Brixen suffered a similar fate. Moreover, 350 mentally ill individuals were murdered, and other mentally and physically handicapped persons "disappeared" from South Tyrolean villages.

May 1945: U.S. troops at the Brenner border.

In 1944, a so-called police transit camp — known as the Sigmundskron concentration camp in common parlance — was set up just outside of Bozen. Up through May 1945, approximately 11,000 persons passed through this camp on their way to the major concentration camps at Mauthausen, Dachau and Auschwitz. Executions were also carried out in the camp itself, which held up to 4,000 prisoners at times.

The Church in South Tyrol showed a willingness to compromise with the new masters, but its approach was cautious. Bishop Geisler made the effort to palliate measures hostile to the Church and to work out a *modus vivendi* with Gauleiter Hofer. Individual priests were indeed arrested; nevertheless, the persecution of the Church never reached the same level it did in North Tyrol where a full 20 percent of all priests were incarcerated at least once.

Resistance

There was little resistance against National Socialism by the South Tyroleans, which was thoroughly understandable since, after all, they had nothing against German rule, though there was indeed opposition to Nazi ideology. In the rest of Italy, of course, national liberation from foreign domination supplied the most powerful motivation for resistance against the Germans. This element was completely absent in South Tyrol for obvious historical, ethnic, and political reasons. Moreover, National Socialist rule meant the reinstatement of a number of basic rights for the South Tyroleans.

The resistance operated in parallel fashion: on the Italian side, there was a group affiliated with the *Comitato di Liberazione Nazionale* (CLN) working in Bozen as well; on the German side, there was the *Andreas-Hofer-Bund* (AHB). There were practically no acts of military resistance carried out by either group. Indeed, there were hardly any contacts between them since their aims were so dissimilar: the CLN demanded that South Tyrol stay a part of Italy and that the Brenner border remain intact; the AHB was for a return to Austria.

The AHB had been founded in 1939; thereafter, its core troop consisted of three dozen stayers. They were opposed to resettlement, which they attempted to delay. They also cared for those who had not opted for Germany and maintained contacts with the German authorities (particularly Prefect Karl Tinzl). Their first chairman was Friedl Volgger; after he was arrested, Hans Egarter took his place. As mentioned above, the AHB was for a reunited Tyrol in a democratic Austria. This conception of a new postwar order was expressed in a memorandum composed by Canon Michael Gamper in exile in Florence. In it, he wrote, "A Tyrol reunited with a resurrected, democratic Austria that has been rid of its imperialistic strivings would in the future also be a powerful bulwark against such manifestations as the reemergence of pan-German tendencies." This would become an important argument after the war.

On 3 May 1945, the CLN took over the administration of the province all the way to the Brenner. That same day, *carabinieri* raised the Italian flag there. Italy had reasserted governmental authority over South Tyrol; in Bozen, a government took office that was administering in the name of Italy and was then confirmed in office by the U.S. military. The increasingly anti-German attitude of the CLN then immediately made itself evident, especially in the administrative area. The Bozen *Unterland*, Cortina d'Ampezzo, and Buchenstein were separated from the Province of Bozen and assigned to the provinces of Trient or Belluno. In many communities, former Fascist Party members were reinstalled as mayors, and there was also a general re-Italianization or re-Fascistification of the bureaucracy. The result was a direct continuation of the Fascist policymaking of the past although Tolomei did no longer play a part in this.

Following liberation, the Italian government suggested to Tolomei that it might be a good idea for him to withdraw from politics and turn over the management of the *Archivio* to Carlo Battisti. Tolomei spent the last years of his life at his countryseat in Glen. He died in 1952 at the age of eighty-six, convinced that his actions had provided a long-term assurance that South Tyrol would remain Italian. Correspondingly grand were the honors showered upon him at his funeral which are still being accorded today by the supporters of the Alleanza Nazionale, the neo-fascists who formerly made up the *Movimento Sociale Italiano* (MSI, or Italian Neofascists) — they see to it that there is always a fresh wreath on his grave.

The Founding of the South Tyrolean People's Party (SVP)

The South Tyrolean People's Party (SVP, or Südtiroler Volkspartei) was founded on 8 May 1945 in the Villa Malfèr in Bozen by a handful of courageous men under the leadership of Bozen businessman Erich Amonn. The founding of the party, at least as far as its substantive orientation was concerned, was no "sudden brainstorm," but the logical continuation of activities of this nature that stayers had already begun during the war years. In late 1942, Erich Amonn had already succeeded in traveling under a pretext to Switzerland where he met with representatives of the Austrian resistance. Following the overthrow of Mussolini in July 1943, a group of South Tyrolean resistance members met at the mountain resort of Ritten near Bozen for talks that had been initiated by an envoy from North Tyrol. Preparatory measures were to be taken in light of a possible end of the war; it was proposed that Canon Gamper leave South Tyrol and establish contact with the Allies south of the "Goth Line," the southern defending line of the *Wehrmacht* north of Rome. Shortly thereafter, Gamper fled; in his hideout near Florence, he composed the previously mentioned memorandum on the South Tyrol problem, the major points of which were later adopted by the SVP. Among them was the following: "South Tyrol is to be reunited with the Province of Tyrol and become incorporated into a reestablished Austria."

When the party was founded in Bozen, Erich Amonn was elected chairman, Josef Menz-Popp, a Burggraf farmer and former Christian Social representative in the provincial legislature, was made vice-chairman, and Josef Raffeiner party secretary. Friedl Volgger joined this group as soon as he returned from Dachau concentration camp and was named organization leader. At their start-up meeting, the founders agreed to three programmatic points that were printed in the daily newspaper *Dolomiten* when it resumed publication on 19 May:

> "1. To fight for the recognition of the cultural, linguistic and economic rights of the South Tyroleans on the basis of democratic principles after twenty-five years of oppression by Fascism and National Socialism.
>
> 2. To help bring peace and order to this land.
>
> 3. To empower its representatives – foreswearing the use of all illegal methods – to advocate before the Allied Powers the claim of the South Tyrolean people to exercise its right of self-determination."

Most important was the third point, in which the SVP quite explicitly demanded the right of self-determination for South Tyrol. As a follow-up to the activities undertaken during the period leading up to 8 May, this demand meant nothing other than the reunification with Tyrol as part of newly established Austria.

VI. 1945/46: South Tyrol and the Cold War

14 September 1945: No Return to Austria

After the Foreign Ministers' Conference in Moscow in October 1943, the Allied governments had called Austria "the first free country to fall a victim to Hitlerite aggression" and had announced their intention of establishing "a free and independent Austria." This became known as the now famous Moscow Declaration. In furtherance of this aim it was thought desirable upon the collapse of Germany to detach Austria from Germany as rapidly as possible. As early as May 1944, the British thought it necessary to agree with the United States and Soviet governments on a territorial definition of Austria. While the most convenient arrangement would no doubt be to restore initially the frontiers laid down in 1919, it was recognized that these included several debatable areas, the most important of which was South Tyrol. On 18 May 1944, the Ministerial Armistice and Postwar Committee of the British War Cabinet discussed this question for the first time and approved the proposals put forward by Minister of State Richard Law. For the immediate purpose of the application of the surrender terms, Law argued, Austria should be defined as in 1937, but, he added,

> we do not, however, rule out the later return to Austria of (i) South Tyrol (ii) Tarvis and the surrounding territory ceded to Italy in 1919. And that while the final disposal of these territories must await the final Peace Settlement, it is desirable that Italian administration and jurisdiction should not be restored in these areas on the eviction of the Germans from Italy and that they should be placed instead under the same form of Allied administration pending the decision as to their future.

This was the British view for the next twelve months. In the Draft Peace Treaty with Italy of April 1945, Section III — South Tyrol — states:

Italy to renounce in favour of the Four Powers all rights and titles in and over the province of Bolzano. In the event of the province being ceded to Austria, Italy to accept the decision of the Boundary Commission which will be established by the Principal Allied Powers to lay down the frontier between Italy and Austria in this region.[20]

This wording was only slightly altered in the version of 9 May 1945. Only the half-sentence "in the event of the province being ceded to Austria" was not included,[21] still not ruling out the return of this province to Austria.

A few weeks later, everything had changed. In the final version of the Draft Peace Treaty of 5 July 1945, Section III was omitted, and no provision for the disposal of this area was made. Foreign Secretary Anthony Eden mentioned the industrialization which had been carried out by the Italians in South Tyrol which had strengthened the economic links between the province and the rest of Italy; maintenance of the existing frontier would thus cause the least economic dislocation. He added that, if the frontier were to be changed, such dislocation would not be serious, given the goodwill between the two countries. He then made it clear that the decision in fact was "really one of high policy," and he asked the decisive question, "Have we more to gain, in the long-term view, by avoiding the further humiliation of Italy or by satisfying Austrian aspirations?"[22] He himself gave the answer:

> I incline to the first alternative. The acquisition of Bolzano cannot be said to be indispensable to a free and independent Austria to which His Majesty's government is committed, and it might on the other hand be a source of danger in the event of Austria falling under purely Russian influence.[23]

Italy was now far more important than Austria; it "must be regarded as a bastion of Anglo-Saxon democracy in the centre of Europe," as the British ambassador in Rome, Noël Charles, put it. For that purpose, he said, "we must be prepared to use the same methods for keeping communism down in Italy as the Russians are using in order to have their views prevail in this country, i.e. supporting clandestinely one particular party with weapons of propaganda, finance and steel."[24]

This was in line with Eden's ideas about Italy. When his paper on Italy was discussed by the Cabinet on 12 July 1945, he asked his colleagues to endorse it and, in addition, to agree upon the following outline of British general policy towards Italy: Great Britain should aim at transforming Italy into a useful member of the European comity of nations, and should lead her to look to the west rather than to the east. To this end, she should be encouraged to provide herself with a government elected on western democratic principles. To empower Italy to enact this policy, Great Britain and the United States would have to help Italy politically and economically. The Cabinet gave general approval to that. South Tyrol was not even mentioned.[25]

This position did not change when the new Labor government took over. Although it appeared from informal conversations with U.S. State Department officials that the U.S. government was in favor of transferring the province of Bolzano, that proved to be wrong. The new British Foreign Secretary Ernest Bevin was still disposed to think, as he told the Cabinet, "that we stand to gain more in the long view by leaving this province to Italy." But if in the course of the Council of Foreign Ministers' first meeting in September in London strong arguments were advanced on the other side, he wanted to have latitude to agree to the cession of this province to Austria. He did not propose to take the initiative in raising this matter, and he saw no reason to include any provision about Bolzano in the Draft Peace Treaty with Italy.[26]

Three days later, ambassador Noël Charles ("I should like to go on record again") once more recommended that Bolzano should not be detached from Italy:

> Political aspects [are] . . . almost decisive. The psychological effect on Italian people . . . would be little short of disastrous. . . With a large Italian population still in the territory and Bolzano city very largely an Italian town, it would undoubtedly give birth to an irredentist movement and fan the flame of nationalism in such a way as to be a sure source of trouble in the future. The fact that 17 percent of hydro-electric power industry of the north (rising at certain periods of the year to a much

higher proportion) would be handed over to Italy's traditional enemy whose policy in the future might be largely directed by the Soviets, would aggravate the above tendency. For above reasons, I feel that pressure on the part of other powers to cede the province to Austria should be resisted, it being understood of course that Italy should give adequate guarantees for local autonomy.[27]

There was no need to resist pressure from the other powers. As it turned out, they all thought along the lines of the British. Thus, on 14 September 1945, the Council of Foreign Ministers (CFM) accepted, without discussion, an American proposal to the effect that Italy's frontier with Austria "would be unchanged, subject to hearing any case Austria may present for minor rectification in her favor."[28]

This thirty-second decision was of historic importance; it should not be changed. It was made in spite of the many manifestations of the Tyroleans' desire in July and August 1945 to be reunited. The newly founded South Tyrolean People's Party (*Südtiroler Volkspartei*, or SVP) was very active,[29] as was the governor (*Landeshauptmann*) of North Tyrol, Karl Gruber (who in October became Austria's Foreign Minister). He appealed to the Allies and asked for "freedom to be restored in South Tyrol, the country of Andreas Hofer after twenty-six years of a cruel oppression that did not even spare the graveyards."[30] In a mass demonstration in Innsbruck on 4 September in favor of reuniting Tyrol, he repeated this appeal.

At the same time the Italian government was very busy. The president of the Italian Council of Ministers, Ferruccio Parri, and Foreign Minister Alcide De Gasperi stated their case for the preservation of the Brenner frontier to U. S. President Harry S. Truman and Secretary of State James Byrnes. First, Italy had built huge electric power plants in the district, those in the provinces of Bolzano and Trento represented 13 percent of the whole national output. Second, an intense sympathy with Nazism penetrated the German-speaking population before and during the war so that the region gave a conspicuous contribution of volunteers to the SS. Thus Parri and De Gasperi warned that the creation of a German "enclave" on the Italian side of the Brenner Pass would be "equivalent to establishing a cradle of future German nationalism, pioneered by those SS-bands which were still roaming on the Alpine slopes." Third, they did not accept the argument that the conservative element in Austria would be strengthened by adding to that country about 200,000 Southern Tyroleans, for they were convinced that either it would be possible to set up a large and economically sound Danubian State, in which case the annexation of a few Tyroleans would be superfluous, or else a small and anemic Austria could only subsist as the protectorate of a great power closely interested in the Danubian Basin. De Gasperi asked the question, "Should the Italian minorities of the Bolzano Province and the economic interest of the whole of Italy be sacrificed to this uncertain future? And, moreover, does this precarious outlook warrant the doors of the Brenner Pass to be left wide open to a new German '*Drang nach Süden*' [thrust to the south]?"[31] There were no such demonstrations from the Austrian government. It was still a provisional Government, not yet recognized by the Western Powers who looked upon this government as a Soviet puppet-government because the old socialist Karl Renner had been installed as chancellor in April 1945 by the Soviets without consulting their western allies, the United States and the United Kingdom. At the government's meeting on 5 September the South Tyrol question was discussed for the first time. The cabinet made it clear that

1. the fate of South Tyrol was of world interest;
2. Tyrol had formed an ethnic and political unit since earliest times;
3. the separation would provide a continuous source of friction with Italy;
4. under existing conditions in Europe, the northern frontier of Italy no longer required strategic safeguards.; and
5. forthcoming peace negotiations with Italy should include the free plebiscite in South Tyrol.[32]

A memorandum following these lines signed by Chancellor Renner, and dated 11 September 1945, was presented to the High Commissioners in Vienna on 12 September 1945. The Austrian Baron von Engert, in presenting this memorandum, asked the British Commission to excuse his method of approach. Since the Provisional Government was not recognized by the three Western Powers, and since Austria was not a member of the United Nations, this unofficial approach was, he explained, the only means open to the Austrian nation of putting their case forward for consideration.[33]

It took ten days until, at last, on 22 September 1945, this memorandum reached the Foreign Office. "Austria's case for recovery of the Alto Adige seems to a great extent to have gone by default," as Michael F. Cullis, head of the Austrian desk in the German Department, recorded on 25 September, and he continued, "Dr. Renner's intervention comes rather too late to be effective."[34] B.A.B. Burrows, first secretary in the Foreign Office, added, "Austria will be able to claim 'minor modifications' of the frontier in her favor. Much will depend on the definition of 'minor.'"[35]

In Rome and Vienna, the Battle Continues

Neither the Italian nor the Austrian government were informed of the CFM decision of 14 September, so in Austria and Italy the battle for South Tyrol continued. The Austrian demand had the support of all parties and the public and was put forward in various forms. Renner made it clear that the South Tyrol question was the "most burning question for Austria." A mass demonstration took place in Vienna on 3 October 1945. It concluded with a resolution appealing to the Allies to repair an injustice and return South Tyrol to Austria. On 5 November, the government sent another memorandum to the Allied Council; on 21 January 1946, Foreign Secretary Gruber sent a memorandum to the Allied Council, followed by a personal letter to Bevin and a similar one by Chancellor Leopold Figl and the Chairman of the SVP. On 6 February 1946 it was Renner's turn; he signed his memorandum not only as a newly elected "Federal President of the Austrian Republic," but also as "former Chairman of the Austrian Delegation at the peace negotiations at Saint-Germain" which had occurred twenty-seven years ago. This well-prepared memorandum was accompanied by personal letters to Truman, British Prime Minister Clement Attlee, French President Félix Gouin, and Josef Stalin. The one to Stalin was particularly cordial; he called the Soviet dictator "Dear Comrade Stalin," the "most outstanding personality and the greatest statesman in our time." On 30 April 1946, the Austrian government prepared another memorandum for circulation to all members of the Peace Conference in Paris.

These diplomatic activities were accompanied by several demonstrations throughout Austria. One of the largest took place at Easter in Innsbruck. "Such a native demonstration as is now to be seen in few places in the world" as *The Times* reported on 23 April, and the paper continued, "It had all the color, dignity and gaiety of the peasant people with a local life stretching back into the Middle Ages, and might almost have been taking place in another age."

A giant petition was presented to Chancellor Figl which bore the signatures of more than 150,000 South Tyroleans, collected secretly and with great difficulty. Figl made a spirited appeal for the return of South Tyrol. The main point in his speech resembled those already made on previous occasions.

The following arguments were the principal points the Austrians put forward in all their memoranda:

1. The award of South Tyrol to Italy after World War I was indefensible and justified solely on strategic grounds, that is, control of the Brenner Pass.
2. The population of the province was predominantly German by race and strongly Austrian by sentiment; the patriotism of the Tyroleans had become indeed proverbial internationally.
3. South and North Tyrol were essentially one unit: separation created intolerable economic, communication, and numerous other difficulties for each. North Tyrol was consequently so isolated that it was easily drawn into the German orbit. For instance, the main road between North Tyrol and Carinthia passed through what was now Italian Tyrol. Tyrol should be looked upon as a European bridge between the East and the West. If South Tyrol was Austrian, it would be possible to join Paris and Budapest without passing through German and Italian territory, via Zürich, Bolzano, and Villach, once the Ofen Pass railway was completed.
4. If the province were detached from Italy, Italian economic interests could easily be safeguarded by:
5. a grant of special status for the hydro-electric plants which would remain Italian property and continue to supply power to Italy at current rates,
6. the establishment of mixed Austro-Italian companies for the joint development of water power, and

7. the provision of additional trade advantages to Italy.
8. The Brenner Pass was no better strategically than the southern boundary of South Tyrol.
9. The Italian record in Tyrol from 1920-43 was a peculiarly black one — already before the Fascist regime.

The principal points the Italians put forward in several memoranda between November 1945 and April 1946 were:

1. The province was given to Italy as a reward for her services in World War I in order to provide her with a strong strategic frontier.
2. Italy fought on the right side for the whole of World War I and for one and three quarter years in World War II; Austria fought on the wrong side for the whole duration of both wars.
3. Between the 1943 Armistice and 1945 VE Day, the Austrians behaved in a peculiarly brutal way towards the Italians in the province.
4. Italy had initiated a policy of cultural and linguistic autonomy in South Tyrol.
5. Industry in northern Italy was greatly dependent on the power supplied by the hydro-electric plants built by the Italians in South Tyrol in the last twenty years.
6. The province was rich in natural resources (aluminum, timber, and so forth) essential to Italy's economy.
7. If, on top of the loss of the colonies and of part of Venezia Giulia, South Tyrol was also detached, no self-respecting Italian government would ever be found to sign a peace treaty so unconscionably harsh in its terms.
8. If the British and the Americans supported the detachment of the province from Italy, irreparable harm would be done to Anglo/American-Italian relations.[36]

There was no spirit of accommodation on the Italian side in those months. Count Sforza, who was the foreign minister in 1920/21 and again from 1947 to 1951 and was now President of the Consulta, was quoted as an illustration of Italian feelings toward Austria: "Austria is a German country and will return to Germany. Let us remember that the most horrible murders were committed by Austrian Nazis.

We must remain united in the face of the constantly threatening danger of the German hordes who will always try to move toward the Mediterranean."[37]

Second Thoughts in Washington and London

The British and the Americans soon had second thoughts about the CFM's decision of September 1945. Events in Austria developed much faster and more favorably than was expected. The most important event was the general elections in November 1945, in which the Communists suffered a humiliating defeat (5.41 percent, four seats out of 165, with eighty-five seats for the conservative People's Party, and seventy-six seats for the Socialists). Austria had decisively rejected Communism. Should the West review the decision of last summer? Should the West make the preservation of Austria a basic aim of postwar Anglo-American policy in preference, if necessary, to attracting Italy to the West?

This question was an extremely difficult one and aroused the strongest feelings, both in the State Department and in the Foreign Office. In the State Department, people like James Riddleberger (Chief of the Division of Central European Affairs) and Samuel Reber (Acting Chief of the Division of Southern European Affairs) held different views. Riddleberger quoted from a draft U.S. memorandum of June 1944 in which the return of Bolzano to Austria had been recommended, a decision which would weaken Italy economically but would strengthen Austria and a "western orientation in this country." Riddleberger therefore recommended that in the forthcoming negotiations the United States should take the position that the Austro-Italian frontier "be rectified by the cession of Bolzano to Austria."[38]

Reber strongly opposed this position, with arguments similar to those of the Italians, and concluded, "Many of the present advocates in Bolzano of Austrian claims were staunch Nazis . . . and Austria therefore does not deserve consideration at the expense of Italy, a cobelligerent."[39] Dean Acheson, acting secretary of state, was not very happy with the contrasting proposals and made his position clear, "I think EUR should settle its difficulties within (repeat within) the family. If you mugs can't reach an agreed position, Doc & I will arbitrate and EUR [Office of European Affairs in the State

Department] will present a united position on this."⁴⁰ Reber and Riddleberger then put forward a joint memorandum that emphasized that the United States should not take the initiative in this question, but if someone else should, the United States would not rule out the holding of a plebiscite.⁴¹ In a note to Freeman H. Matthews, the director of EUR, Reber made it clear that he had initiated this because he felt it was theoretically the best solution but did so with serious misgivings: 1.) chiefly, he did not believe that any Italian government would sign a peace treaty ceding Bolzano to Austria, and 2.) he was not sure what effect this would have on the previous decisions by the CFM.⁴²

A plebiscite was exactly what the Austrian government had asked for, but, as Charles Cope in the Foreign Office made clear, a plebiscite was undesirable "since it would not tell us anything that we did not already know and it would only serve to embitter suspicions that already divide each Tyrolean village."⁴³

Discussion of the whole problem started in early January 1946 when Cope, commenting on the Austrian memorandum of 5 November (which was received in the Foreign Office on 27 December), accepted the Austrian argument that 1.) the South Tyroleans were pro-Austrian, 2.) the historic claim was valid, 3.) the Brenner frontier never existed until 1919, and 4.) that the communication claim was also valid. To him, the merits of the case, therefore, pointed to the return of South Tyrol to Austria provided that satisfactory economic arrangements were made. But certain wider considerations had been taken into account before the return of South Tyrol could completely be endorsed. It would certainly have far-reaching effects, including those:

> a. on Austria, which would be better able to achieve real independence and security; it would tend to orient Austria away from the Danube and the East and towards the West and the South. It would also strengthen the chances of economic security and "should thereby reduce the dangers of Communism"; and

> b. on Italy, which equally attached great importance to the retention of South Tyrol. To Cope it was questionable, however, whether this emphasis on retaining South Tyrol was equally

genuine and deep seated. If Italy retained Trieste, she "might resign herself to the loss of Bolzano."⁴⁴

What about the British interests? There would be a stronger Austria, but one still requiring continuous support, and an Italy, cross and chastened, requiring all the more support to be kept on an even keel. If Austria was allowed to slip back into her prewar insecurity, Cope was afraid that she might be forced to rely on a power hostile to a Western Bloc in an attempt to make good her claims, for example, the Soviet Union or a renascent Germany. Indirectly, the restoration of South Tyrol, by strengthening Austrian self-confidence, would make a future annexation less likely. On balance, this restoration would help Austria more than it would harm Italy, assuming always that Italy kept Trieste. Cope then suggested taking the question to the Cabinet because

> . . . this seems to be one of the few cases in which the peace treaty can alter frontiers in accordance with the wishes of the population. That alone should recommend the restoration. Ethnic problems tend to be constant. Questions of expediency are always in flux and it is difficult therefore now to state whether British interests over a long period would be better served by giving South Tyrol to Italy or to Austria. At the moment anyway there is at least as good an argument of expediency for the return of the province to Austria as for its retention by Italy. We might thus advocate its return.⁴⁵

Lord Samuel Hood in the Foreign Office accepted that justice was certainly a sounder basis for policy than expediency, but he warned that "in a case like this the ardor with which we pursue justice must be influenced by an appreciation of our own interests." He thought it desirable to review the CFM decision, but identified the need for an objective approach to the whole question. He doubted that the cession of South Tyrol to Austria by itself would establish Austrian independence for all time. To achieve this result, continuous effort over a long period would be necessary, but if this effort could only be made at the expense of starving Italy one could succeed in creating an island of true democracy in Central Europe, but an island fated ultimately to be engulfed by the surrounding flood of

Communism. On the other hand, if it was possible to support Italy *and* Austria, then the latter would no longer be an island but a most valuable peninsula. Reason as well as justice would then point to giving Austria South Tyrol "and we should not be deterred by the tears of the Italians who will be bound to us anyway by the strongest of bonds: self-interest."

A.D.M. Archibald Ross warned that if Bolzano was taken away from Italy it would look as though the West was punishing her not only for losing the last war but also for having been on the winning side in the one before, "while we reward Austria for having fought and lost two wars against us." To John Troutbeck, Head of the German Department, it seemed very silly to adopt a partisan attitude, on either side. Although justice obviously lay with the Austrians, that was no reason for overstating their case:

> I do not believe that the return of this region to Austria would strengthen her security or make a future Anschluß less likely. Nor have I any faith in Austria standing out against any wave that might sweep over Central Europe, be it Communism or new-Fascism or anything else. She is too small and her people to irresolute to form a bulwark without strong outside support, and it is difficult to see from where it should come.[46]

But to prolong an injustice, which would always remain a point of soreness and irritation, seemed to him a mistake, and one that would do no good even to Italy, and he came to the conclusion, "Our vote should be on the Austrian side." Under-Secretary of State Oliver Harvey agreed, whereas his colleague Frederick Hoyer-Millar wanted to deal with this problem largely from the point of view of

> ... what is in fact best in our own interests. If we do not want to defeat our long-term Italian policy, we must not make our peace with Italy too harsh. Otherwise, especially as the B*r*enner frontier has become a kind of fetish to the Italians there is a real risk that the Italian Government will refuse to sign the treaty, and that a period of confusion will ensue, during which Italy would surely tend to lose heart and turn towards Russia.[47]

Looked at purely from the point of view of justice, there was nevertheless no reason why Italy should be allowed to continue to govern those "unwilling Germans in South Tyrol," as Sir Orme Sargent, permanent under-secretary of state in the Foreign Office, put it in a memo for Foreign Minister Ernest Bevin, "They were handed over to them in 1919 as a matter of power politics and for no other reason. At the time it was considered a scandal, and if we perpetuate this injustice now, I feel certain we shall be laying up trouble for Europe later on." For him the only safe tactic was to apply the ethnic principle strictly, while making all necessary provisions for safeguarding Italian participation in the hydraulic power derived from this region. This, he thought, could be done quite easily without handing over the inhabitants to Italian administration.

No doubt, Italian *amour propre* would be wounded by the loss of territories that the peace treaty would impose upon them. But to mitigate this, Sargent thought it far better to do so by giving back to the Italians one of their colonies rather than by handing this German population over to them.

South Tyrol would go back to Austria! This was the result of a meeting of all the interested Departments of the Foreign Office on 24 January. This was, nevertheless, not the end of the story. Bevin was not sure whether reviewing the CFM's decision was the right approach, as his comment "I must give this more consideration" showed. Hoyar-Millar of the pro-Italian lobby in the Foreign Office disagreed with the outcome of the above-mentioned meeting. In his opinion, the Bolzano question was perhaps the issue about which the Italian public felt most strongly, and he warned that it was a matter on which all elements of the country, from extreme right to extreme left, were united. Harvey did not accept this position; his answer was clear enough, "All the same Italy's case in Bolzano is weakest at all." Gladwyn Jebb, the U.K. Deputy at Lancaster House, had second thoughts, too. To him, giving back South Tyrol to Austria was placing the most important card in the hands of the Italian Communists, especially if it were known that the Soviet Union had not approved the transfer. And what would be the corresponding gain?

Future of the South Tyrol.

Looked at purely from the point of view of justice there is no reason why Italy should be allowed to continue to govern these unwilling Germans in the South Tyrol. They were handed over to them in 1919 as a matter of power politics and for no other reason. At the time it was considered a scandal and if we perpetuate this injustice now I feel certain we shall be laying up trouble for Europe later on.

It is quite possible that the Soviet Government will support the Italian claim, but if so they will there again be playing power politics.

Surely the only safe line is to apply strictly the ethnic principle, while making all necessary provisions for safeguarding Italian participation in the hydraulic power derived from this region. This could be done quite easily without handing over the inhabitants to Italian administration.

No doubt Italian amour propre and prestige are going to be wounded by the loss of territories which the peace treaty is going to impose upon them. But if we want to mitigate this I think it would be far better to do so by giving back to the Italians one of their colonies rather than by handing this Germanic population over to them.

If we look beyond prestige and amour propre it is obvious, as pointed out in this paper, that what the Italians need above all things is a guarantee that they will be able to export their surplus population. It must always be remembered that the American decision after the war of 1914-18 to limit immigration into the U.S.A. produced strains and discontents in Italy which were among the causes that eventually led to the Fascist régime.

I would suggest, therefore, that our representative on the Deputies' Committee should be authorised to proceed on the lines indicated in points (i) to (v) of the attached memorandum.

OGSargent

February 8th, 1946.

I must give this more consideration. EB

February 1946: A colony in return for South Tyrol? Minutes by British Foreign Office Permanent Under-Secretary of State Orme Sargent to Foreign Minister Ernest Bevin caused Bevin to note, " I must give this more consideration. EB."

Presumably increased goodwill on the part of the Austrian government. But as long as this government is under the control or influence of Moscow, such goodwill will count for little, supposing that our relations with Russia are strained; whereas, if our relations with Russia are really cordial, Austrian ill-will simply will not matter. In any case, we have much more chance of getting a Western democracy established in Rome than we have of getting one established in Vienna.[48]

Jebb did not pretend that handing back South Tyrol to Austria would be a disaster from the British point of view. He certainly saw some advantages in doing so, especially if one dallied with the dangerous notion that "we may one day have to try to rely on Germanic support against the U.S.S.R." But even in that event Jebb did not suppose that "some future pro-British *Führer* would worry about the *Südtiroler* any more than Adolf Hitler did."

Bevin called a meeting on 4 March to put a final end to the discussion. It was decided that, although in equity the Austrians had the stronger case, Jebb should not support their claim for the return of the whole of South Tyrol. To hand over the power plants to them might in effect provide the Soviets with an effective lever to bring undesirable pressure on Italy. In other words, "This might assist Russian designs in Central Europe and operate against the establishment of a Western democratic regime in Italy." The loss of South Tyrol might upset the Italian government and "open the way for the Communists." Moreover, though the British were doing all they could to stiffen the Austrian Government, they were not sure of final success and worried that "Austria may by the force of things end up gravitating to the east rather than to the west."[49]

The Mediterranean was the area through which the British wanted to bring influence to bear on Southern Europe, the soft underbelly of France, Italy, Yugoslavia, Greece, and Turkey. Without British physical presence in the Mediterranean, "we should cut little ice with these states which would fall, like Eastern Europe, under the totalitarian yoke," as Bevin told the Defense Committee. "If we move out of the Mediterranean, Russia will move in, and the Mediterranean countries, from the point of view of commerce and trade, economy and democracy, will be finished."[50] Under those circumstances, then, Italy should not be weakened by taking away from her South Tyrol. The so-called "Russian danger" had become the focus of British foreign policy in those days. Bevin was sure that the Soviets, as he wrote to Prime Minister Clement Attlee, "have decided upon an aggressive policy based upon militant Communism and Soviet chauvinism and seem determined to stick at nothing, short of war, to obtain her objectives."[51]

As the British decided not to reopen the South Tyrol question, South Tyrol's fate was finally sealed. The Americans and the French were thinking along the lines of the British and showed no disposition to take a pro-Austrian line. The French Government seemed generally sympathetic to Austria, but took up no position. The U.S. government favored Italy mainly because of the powerful Italian vote in America and the administration's feeling that the loss of South Tyrol would be the last straw for Italy and make her unwilling to sign the Peace Treaty. The Soviets, too, were not interested in weakening Italy and the Italian Communist Party, for obvious reasons. They opposed the Austrian claim presumably on account of the rebuff suffered by the Communists in the Austrian election in November 1945 and of the support which it gave to Yugoslavia against Italy over Trieste. At the same time, Moscow wanted to deal a blow to Austria's will for independence in the hope, as the British put it, "that it would fall a readier victim to Communism."[52] Thus, South Tyrol became the first victim in the still undeclared Cold War.

On 1 May 1946, the Council of Foreign Ministers in Paris decided that Austria's request for the return of South Tyrol to Austria could not be regarded as minor rectifications within the meaning of the September decision of 1945. The Council therefore decided that those requests could not be taken into consideration. Publication of the Foreign Ministers' decision led to a general strike in Tyrol on 2 May. A large demonstration occurred in Innsbruck culminating in a procession to the Andreas Hofer monument. Demonstrators carried leaflets bearing slogans such as "Tyrol protests against victory of Hitler and Mussolini." Members of the Tyrolean provincial government took part in the demonstration; the government issued a proclamation registering a "passionate protest against this new violation." In the evening, the French military authorities imposed a curfew. At the same time, there were disturbances in South Tyrol and clashes with Italian gendarmerie in the Pustertal.

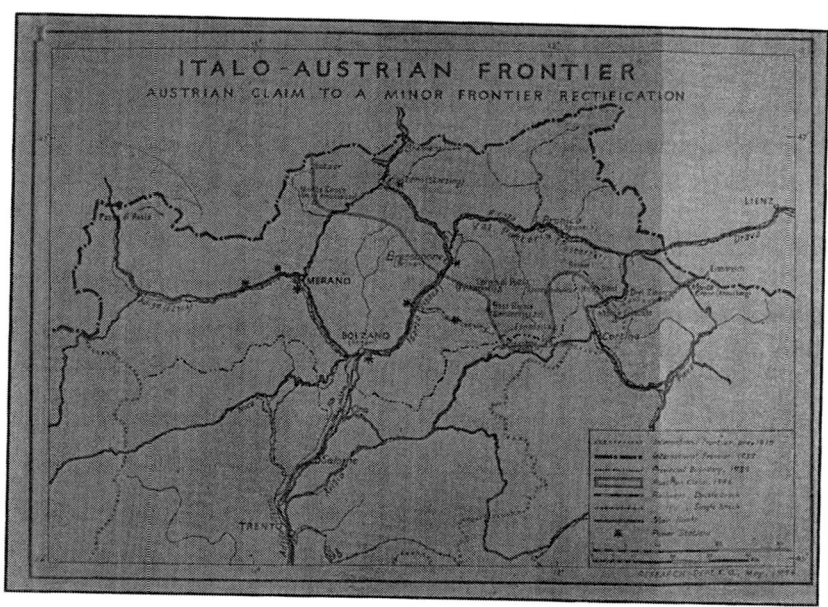

In September 1945, the Allies decide that the Brenner frontier "would be unchanged, subject to hearing any case Austria may present for minor rectification." Austria asks for such a "minor rectification" in May 1946, but the Allies are against it.

The Austrian government then put forward a modified claim for the district of the Pustertal comprising the towns of Bruneck (Brunico) and Brixen (Bressanone) in the northeast corner of the province, and covering some 50,000 of its total population, asking that this area should be returned to Austria as a "minor modification."

The British themselves had urged the Austrians to put forward this claim. They had tried to assess the respective values of various parts of the province to Austria. The letter from President Renner of 8 February had made it clear that the return of the Brunico-Bressanone area, including the railway line linking eastern and northern Tyrol, was of the highest importance. So, if the Pustertal area would be returned to Austria, this would meet one important Austrian argument in restoring direct communication between Innsbruck and the province of Carinthia. It would also restore an appreciable number of German-speaking people to Austria without depriving Italy of any important hydroelectric power stations. It would, however, certainly greatly distress the Italians if they were deprived of the Brenner frontier. This rectification would by no means satisfy the Austrians, and, "sentimentally, no doubt, Austria would mourn the loss of Schloß Tirol and the Andreas Hofer country, and this would also leave inside Italy about 120,000 German and Ladin speaking people." But they would almost certainly regard it as a good deal better than nothing, as one official in the Foreign Office put it.

It was more than that as Foreign Minister Karl Gruber told William Mack, the British representative in Vienna, on 7 May. It was his hope that, if this transfer were made, an arrangement in regard to the rest of South Tyrol might be reached directly with the Italians at a later date, once the Brenner frontier was removed. In other words, as Gladwyn Jebb put it after a talk with Gruber on 4 June in London, "Dr. Gruber evidently thinks ... he will get the Italians on the run and that over a period of years he will succeed in getting the whole of the Alto Adige at any rate incorporated administratively." The Italians would imagine that the Austrians were getting by the back door what had been refused to them by the front door. On the other hand, if the frontier was maintained, there was no doubt that the British government would be subjected to considerable criticism in the House of Commons based largely on the argument that, whereas they had insisted on the application of the ethnic principle in Venezia

Guilia, they had absolutely refused to apply it in the case of South Tyrol. But Gruber's ideas made an already difficult suggestion even more difficult. The dilemma for the British was therefore a real one. For Jebb, the best way out of it seemed to be to suggest that "whereas we ourselves would have been prepared to entertain an Austrian claim to the Pustertal at any rate, the Soviet attitude made this impossible." At least he admitted that this would be "slightly dishonest, of course, ... but it might nevertheless prove to be the easiest way out of the dilemma."[53]

The French were thinking along similar lines, for their delegate in the Council of Deputies, Couve de Murville, made it clear in the sixty-fifth meeting on 7 June. He noted that, if the new Austrian claims were granted, the Austrians would have further demands to make in regard to South Tyrol. In other words, this would not be a final settlement, but only a beginning. In his view, any solution should be final, "in view of the necessity for general European pacification." Interpretations of what might constitute "a minor rectification" could vary, but the main question was "whether the Council wished to award anything to Austria."

Looking to the Soviets, the Western powers were not disappointed. "Russian fear of the Germans using this path to attack what Russia would call her 'vital Mediterranean interests,'" as Bevin put it, showed the way out of the dilemma. The Soviets were against any cession of territory to Austria. Wjatscheslav Molotov proposed a resolution that the Council of Foreign Ministers could not regard the Austrian claims to the Pustertal as "minor rectification" to the Austro-Italian frontier. His western colleagues readily accepted his view on 24 June.

[This telegram is of particular secrecy and should be retained by the authorised recipient and not passed on].

[CYPHER]   SPECIAL (PACS)

VIENNA TO FOREIGN OFFICE

(From British Diplomatic Representative in Austria).

Mr. Nicholls.   D. 4.20 p.m. 13th June 1946.
No. 511.
13th June 1946.   R. 6.50 p.m. 13th June 1946.

YYYYY

IMMEDIATE
SECRET

My telegram No. 510.

Dr. Gruber told me that just before leaving for London he had seen the Italian Ambassador at the latter's request.

Count Carandini had broached the subject of the South Tyrol and had asked whether Dr. Gruber did not think that it might be better to deal with the question by direct negotiation rather than leave it to the Council of Foreign Ministers. Dr. Gruber had replied non-committally that the idea was an interesting one.

5. Dr. Gruber has not yet discussed the matter with his colleagues. He is, however, clearly taken with the idea and envisages a solution under which the two Governments would set up a joint Italo-Austrian Administration under U.N.O. supervision, for the whole area originally claimed by Austria. Italy would retain her economic rights and could station troops on the Brenner, while Austria's cultural requirements and communications would be secured.

5. If the idea appeals to his colleagues Dr. Gruber will work out a concrete scheme and give me a copy for transmission to you. He hopes the Italian Government could then be induced to make the running. He particularly asks that both the Italian Ambassador's approach and his

One of the numerous telegrams from the British representative in Vienna, William H.B. Mack, to the Foreign Office, informing it about the situation in Vienna.

VII. 1946: The Gruber-De Gasperi Agreement

Austrian Foreign Minister Karl Gruber was in a state of deep depression after news of the Paris decision came through. He seemed to think that the Americans and the British had let him down. On 25 June, British representative William Mack tried to encourage him, but without much success.

Austrian Chancellor Leopold Figl took a more realistic view. He told Mack that he firmly believed that South Tyrol would some day return to Austria. Twenty years were nothing in the life of a nation, "it took the French fifty years to get back Alsace Lorraine." Meanwhile, the Austrian government would have to let their compatriots in South Tyrol know that they still regarded them as Austrians. It was essential that the Italian government should be compelled by the Allied powers to subscribe to provisions for proper treatment of the German-speaking element in South Tyrol. A few days later, Mack tried to encourage Gruber to pursue the idea of direct negotiations with the Italian government. The answer was "no," on the grounds that without the Pustertal the Austrians had no cards in their hands and the Italians no inducement to come to a satisfactory arrangement, and, as Mack reported to London, "it is impossible to shake them out of this attitude at present. They continue to receive evidence from all parts of Austria of deep disappointment amounting in some cases almost to despair."

The reports coming in from Vienna showed clearly that the CFM decision had a bad effect on the Austrians and that one of its most unwelcome results, from the British point of view, would undoubtedly be to strengthen the hands of the Communists and other elements who favored a re-orientation of Austria's foreign and domestic policy towards the Soviet Union and the Soviet-controlled bloc in Eastern Europe. More and more people in London felt increasingly unhappy about this turn of events. Bevin had to defend the CFM's decision to a critical House of Commons. Winston

Churchill made it clear that "in the vast confusion of Europe South Tyrol is indeed a touchstone."⁵⁴ Orme Sargent found it curious that

> . . . to justify this violation of the ethnic principle, we are advancing the same argument as was advanced by the peacemakers of 1919, i.e. that we must propitiate Italy because it is essential that she should remain our friend whereas Austria is weak, uncertain and valueless. We did not foresee at that time the advent of Mussolini, nor the value of building up Austria as a rampart against Nazi-aggression in Central Europe.⁵⁵

Looking at the problem for the long-term and European point of view, Sargent regarded it as essential that both countries, situated as they were close to the Iron Curtain, should cling together; he warned:

> Although wise people in Italy and Austria realize this, the two countries as a whole are psychologically incapable of getting and working together, unless they are compelled by the Great Powers to sink their antipathies and to rid themselves of continuing causes of friction, which will otherwise poison their relations indefinitely and do themselves and us nothing but harm.⁵⁶

He was convinced that as long as the Italians and Austrians were left to themselves, nothing would be done. "The Austrians are too weak to force the pace, and the Italians, as *beati possidentes* have no real inducement to conclude any definite agreement."⁵⁷ To Patrick Dean, the newly appointed head of the German Department in the Foreign Office, it was a matter of immediate political expediency, as well as of long-term wisdom, to see whether, "before it is too late, some steps cannot be taken towards reconsidering our attitude over this question."

The time had come for him to take steps to bring Italy and Austria, "these two essentially Western countries," together and produce proposals to get this matter settled quickly in order to prevent both or either the Austrian and Italian governments from becoming dominated by the Communists and the Soviets. He was convinced that the problem was capable of solution along the lines Orme Sargent suggested on 3 August, that is, autonomy for the Bozen

AUSTRIAN DELEGATION
TO THE PARIS CONFERENCE

1° - German speaking inhabitants of the Bolzano Province and of neighbouring bilingual townships of the Trento Province will be assured a complete equality of rights with the Italian-speaking inhabitants, with in the framework of special provisions to safeguard the ethnical character and the cultural and economic development of the German-speaking element.

In accordance with legislation already enacted or awaiting enactment the said German-speaking citizens will be granted in particular:

(a) elementary and secondary teaching in the mother-tongue;
(b) parification of the German and Italian languages in public offices and official documents, as well as in bilingual topographic naming;
(c) the right to re-establish German family names which were italianized in recent years;
(d) equality of rights as regards the entering upon public offices, with a view to reaching a more appropriate proportion of employment between the two ethnical groups.

The Gruber-De Gasperi – or Paris Agreement – signed on 5 September 1946 in Paris by Italy's Prime Minister Alcide De Gasperi and Austria's Foreign Minister Karl Gruber. This text is the original and definitive text. English was one of the official languages at the conference in Paris. Degasperi later changed the spelling of his name to De Gasperi.

- 2 -

2° - The populations of the above mentioned zones will be granted the exercise of an autonomous legislative and executive regional power. The frame within which the said provisions of autonomy will apply, will be drafted in consultation also with local representative German-speaking elements.

3° - The Italian Government, with the aim of establishing good neighbourhood relations between Austria and Italy, pledges itself, in consultation with the Austrian Government and within one year from the signing of the present Treaty:

(a) to revise in a spirit of equity and brod-mindedness the question of the options for citizenship resulting from the 1939 Hitler-Mussolini agreements;

(b) to find an agreement for the mutual recognition of the validity of certain degrees and University diplomas;

(c) to draw up a convention for the free passengers and goods transit between Northern and Eastern Tyrol both by rail and, to the greatest possible extent, by road;

(d) to reach special agreements aimed at facilitating enlarged frontier traffic and local exchanges of certain quantities of characteristic products and goods between Austria and Italy.

5. September 1946

province under Italian sovereignty with considerable guaranteed rights of culture, access, and trade for the German-speaking majority. He did not think it would be easy to reach such a solution, but it was clearly a British interest to do so, since, as Dean feared that, if no solution was reached, the question of South Tyrol would continue to poison Austrian-Italian relations and the only people who were likely to gain from this were the Soviets, who would be able to spread their influence by playing one side off against the other. He thought the best service the British could now give to both sides would be "to help them to forget the murky past and to look to their future together as Western powers."[58]

Autonomy for South Tyrol was the solution! The British made it clear to the Italians that it could not be to Italy's advantage to force Austria into the arms of the Soviets. This British initiative brought about an Italian-Austrian agreement over the next few weeks. What the Italians and Austrians proposed in Paris, the tactical variants of how best to proceed, as well as — and this was of no less importance — how to anchor all this in the peace treaty, was intensively discussed with the English in Paris, even if Italian Prime Minister Alcide De Gasperi and Austrian Foreign Minister Karl Gruber did not then submit the final version of the agreement to them prior to signing.

On 5 September 1946, Gruber and De Gasperi signed the accord that has gone down in history as the Gruber–De Gasperi Agreement, or Paris Agreement or Treaty of Paris. It was written in English, which was one of the conference languages and the one in which the treaty had to be drafted though both politicians were no great masters of the English language, as can be seen in a detail such as there is no such word as "parification." In the copy for the Italians, even the word "peace" is misspelled.

This agreement was amplified and supplemented by an exchange of letters (in English) that same day between De Gasperi and Gruber. De Gasperi confirmed that the Italian government would "be prepared to give careful attention" to any suggenstions from the Austrian government concerning the best solution to implement the agreement. In his answer, Gruber acknowledged receipt of the letter, cited the passage quoted above, and went on to say that he wished to add that the agreement "is viewed by us with real satisfaction," and they very much hoped that it "will be the starting point for a fruitful development of Austro-Italian relations in the spirit of friendly neighbourhood and of international cooperation."

Shaking hands after signing the agreement: Italy's Prime Minister Alcide De Gasperi and Austria's Foreign Minister Karl Gruber on 5 September 1946 in Paris.

In the wording of the "activity report" prepared by the South Tyrolean delegation (three South Tyroleans were present in Paris: Friedl Volgger, Otto von Guggenberg and Hans Schoefl), Gruber attached particularly great weight to De Gasperi's letter, since the Italian government had thereby committed itself to carefully consider any of the Austrian government's proposals having to do with the agreement. In his opinion, the Austrian government was thereby entitled to intervene at any time in any aspect of the autonomy negotiations, as well as to lodge protests at any time thereafter due to inadequate implementation, subsequent restrictions of autonomy, and so forth, without the Italian government being able to dismiss this exertion of influence by Austria.

How did the Italians see this? Which obligations did they assume on the basis of this agreement? Niccolò Carandini, Italy's ambassador in London who played an important role in the discussions in Paris, discussed the answers to these questions in a letter dated 25 September 1946 to Renato Prunas, the General Secretary of the Italian Foreign Ministry. In Carandini's view, what had been signed was

> not a normal treaty that categorically obliged both parties to comply with all points. The first part of the document having to do with certain measures regarding language, etc. is binding for us. The second part, however, is not binding, neither with respect to the substance nor the extent of autonomy. The third part (questions of an international character) is binding as far as the general nature of the measures to be implemented and consultation with the Austrian government is concerned. In general, it is an agreement that was concluded in good faith and which, as Gruber has assured and as the future will show, will prove to be something of value upon which we can rely only when it is implemented in good faith as well.[59]

In Vienna, where the return of South Tyrol had been the sole topic of discussion for months, there was at first some difficulty in properly assessing the agreement, which was a rather complicated document.

As Gruber reported, "The so-called treaty that isn't a treaty" is how the minutes of the 1 October Council of Ministers meeting read. Gruber took it completely for granted that the agreement — which is how he referred to it — was merely a "gentleman's agreement," not a treaty; the actual treaty with all the details worked out would only be concluded at a later date. He thus came across as being more naïve than he actually was. After all, he had signed it as foreign minister and not as a private individual. Later, no one had any doubts as to whether a treaty had been signed; nevertheless, it is certainly interesting to note that the agreement was neither ratified by the Austrian Parliament (which even the Foreign Office's experts in international law had deemed necessary) nor published in the Austrian Federal Law Gazette. The only action taken was a resolution adopted by Parliament's Foreign Affairs Committee on 1 October 1946 stating that the "settlement" concluded with Italy, although it was not clear whether it had won the approval of the entire South Tyrolean people, still needed "a good deal of interpretation in order to be accepted as an interim solution." The Committee went on to say:

> Austria's stance is by no means to be interpreted as a renunciation of our state's inalienable rights to South Tyrol. The Committee gives expression to the resolute hope that a changed international situation will in the future make it possible for the South Tyroleans themselves to determine their state affiliation.

This principle was said to be "the only way to achieve a long-term solution of the South Tyrol question" that "could be accepted as just and satisfactory" by Austria. Such boundless enthusiasm certainly raised expectations of possible resolutions to the South Tyrol question! Only after a time did people realize that this was an extremely important agreement, a kind of Magna Carta for South Tyrol. From now on, South Tyrol was an international affair and no longer Italy's internal affair, for the agreement was part of the Allied Peace Treaty with Italy; and Austria had thereby gotten the right to "protect" South Tyrol. Without this agreement, it would not have been possible to take the case to the United Nations as Austria did in 1960.

From the very start, one of the most divisive points in the interpretation of the agreement was Article 2 and the territorial demarcation of the autonomous region, the famous "frame." Here, however, Italy presented a *fait accompli* in June 1947 by enacting a constitution that, in Article 108, provided for the formation of an autonomous region Trentino-Alto Adige (Trentino-Tiroler Etschland), and passing the corresponding autonomy legislation in January 1948. This was not autonomy for the land of South Tyrol! Is this what had been agreed upon in Paris? The territorial delimitation of the autonomous region was the centerpiece of the agreement; the inclusion of Trentino would "upset everything," as Figl said to the Council of Ministers on 17 September 1946. Particularly in this question, one could truly have expected that things would have been made crystal clear with no room left for divergent interpretations, but what transpired was the exact opposite, and indeed — as the records show — for good reason. The files also show that in Paris there had been no unclear points between Gruber and De Gasperi, between Austrians and Italians, in this respect; nevertheless, in consideration of public opinion in Austria and Italy, things could not be spelled out so clearly. One could well ask why De Gasperi had even signed the agreement in Paris. Nothing and nobody could have forced him to do so, not even the British. The South Tyrolean delegates themselves spoke of De Gasperi having made "voluntary" commitments.

De Gasperi wanted to bring calm to the Brenner, to get the demand for a "Break with Rome!" out of the headlines of the international press once and for all, and to achieve autonomy for "his" people of Trentino. For this, he was ready to pay a price, and that was his signature in Paris. Once the "South Tyrol game" had finally lost its allure among the major powers, Gruber wanted at least an internationally guaranteed commitment from Italy establishing Italian recognition of Austria's role as protector of South Tyrol and simultaneously settling the *Optanten* question. To achieve this goal, a price had likewise to be paid. For one thing, the demand for self-determination and the return of South Tyrol to Austria had to be honored, but could not take place publicly, although this is precisely what the agreement meant. This resolution was something that some in North Tyrol as well as in South Tyrol and Vienna could not accept. For them, the agreement was merely an interim solution, which naturally raised the question: To what sort of final solution would this interim solution lead? Would self-determination finally be granted one day? In 1960-61, this question would assume rather dramatic proportions. Moreover, Gruber had to accept what De Gasperi was prepared to give if he wished to avoid returning from Paris empty-handed. If he had departed from Paris under protest — which would certainly have been a possibility — then the South Tyroleans would have remained completely defenseless, and Austria would not have assumed the mantle of "protective power" (although it was not until the second half of the 1950s that it could play this role actively). To achieve his goal, Gruber at times played a daring game; in doing so, he never really laid his cards on the table, even when he had cards to play. Nowhere is this as clear as in the question of the territorial demarcation of the autonomous region. In Paris, the initial positions of the Italians, the Austrians, and the South Tyroleans on this point were totally clear. In the plan worked out by Bozen Prefect Silvio Innocenti, South Tyrol and Trentino were to become an interconnected autonomous region. In this case, though, the South Tyroleans would have constituted a minority to such an extent that it would no longer even have been possible to speak of genuine autonomy for South Tyrol (200,000 South Tyroleans versus 500,000 Italians).

It was well-known that De Gasperi, himself a native of Trentino, had promised autonomy to the people of his region — who harbored separatist tendencies — and thus for domestic political reasons wished for an *ad hoc* alliance or even unification of the provinces of Bozen and Trient.

According to Ambassador Carandini, Gruber was prepared to leave the question of geographic boundaries open, but he preferred a more general formulation. He ultimately accepted Carandini's suggestion, which was also adopted in the subsequent agreement and read as follows, "The frame within which the said provisions of autonomy will apply, will be drafted in consultation also with local representative German-speaking elements."

Gruber wanted only to eliminate the word "also." Carandini referred to the Constitutional Convention, which, quite reasonably, would be the first to express an opinion here; then, together with Italian-speaking groups, German-speaking representatives would "also" be consulted. Gruber agreed to this proposal.

On 24 September 1964, Gruber held a breakfast meeting with Carandini in a private dining room at the Restaurant Drouant in Paris, which Austrian Ambassadors Heinrich Schmid, Norbert Bischoff and Lothar Wimmer (Carandini: "Witnesses to all of our agreements") also attended. The following day, Carandini reported to Secretary General Prunas about what transpired:

> I had the opportunity to clarify once again with complete and absolute openness the gist of our agreement and the intentions of those with whom it was concluded. I told Gruber and the others:
>
> 1. We have signed an agreement of a unilateral nature, whereby we commit ourselves to grant autonomy without demanding in return an express declaration of disclaimer waiving your territorial claims. This was done in order to avoid putting you in a difficult position *vis-à-vis* your nationalistic public opinion. It

is true that your waiver proceeds from the fact that you dropped all previous claims at the conference. It is true that the incorporation of our agreement into the peace treaty makes the Italian-Austrian question, which was raised at the conference as a result of a territorial claim and which was likewise resolved there by granting autonomy to the minority group in question, an international affair. But what are your thoughts on this matter?

Gruber explained to me: 'On the day when the autonomy question is resolved and the wishes of the German-speaking minority are thereby satisfied, South Tyrol will be a closed case for Austria.'

2. As far as the territorial extent is concerned, I pointed out (and I really have to force myself to address this issue again for the umpteenth time) the necessity — since this is, after all, a matter for which I bear a share of the responsibility — to hear from him once again that there are no misunderstandings about this question having been left open. I wanted a final explanation in order to inform Prime Minister De Gasperi. Gruber gave me comprehensive and clear assurance, and reiterated that the decision depended upon us and that he would make every effort to see to it that this matter would be concluded with as few difficulties and as much harmony as possible. For tactical reasons, he asked me to avoid for a time embarrassing him in front of his nationalistically-oriented public, whereby he would have to openly acknowledge an obligation that — although it clearly arises from the application of the 'in the framework of ...' formula — he had accepted because he trusted our discretion. And he stated all of this in a very explicit tone. If, under these conditions, I were now to write him a letter asking him to publicly reaffirm his explanation in one way or another, I would not only embarrass him but also perhaps put him in the predicament of having to give me a vague answer, which would not go beyond the content of the treaty as signed, would also not place him under any obligations beyond that, and would not expose him to direct domestic attacks, the avoidance of which is in both of our interests.[60]

Otto von Guggenberg, one of the three South Tyrolean representatives in Paris, had problems similar to Prunas', though indeed for different reasons. He too wanted a precise formulation, and asked Gruber on 23 September to set down his assurances in writing, "since passing this on by word of mouth could easily lead to misconceptions, and, above all, to doubts on our part." Thus on 24 September following his breakfast with Carandini, Gruber composed his now-famous letter to von Guggenberg. In the decisive passage, Gruber wrote what he had explained to De Gasperi:

> Any solution to which the South Tyroleans would freely agree without having been subjected to any pressure would also receive Austria's approval. We nevertheless had to request that the text be worded in such a way that the geographical extent of this autonomous region would also require the consent of the South Tyroleans. We agreed in writing to the word "frame," the meaning of which is made clear in the context of the discussion when it is employed in conjunction with the word "consultation" that occurs in the same sentence.[61]

At talks held two days later in Innsbruck with representatives of North and South Tyrol, Gruber elaborated on the reasons for direct negotiations and the final accord with Italy. He named three:

> 1. In case of a break with Italy, South Tyrol could not count on receiving aid or support from Austria for at least two years, since Austria is involved in a struggle for its own existence. Help for South Tyrol would have to come from the major powers, which would not be favorably disposed to Austria in the case of a break. In South Tyrol, which would then be at the mercy of the Italians, a split in the party would then certainly occur, since a significant faction within it would definitely seek to cooperate with the Italians.

> 2. It is true that one could have returned home with a flaming protest and this protest could perhaps be revived in two or three years; in the meantime, though, things would have happened in South Tyrol that would not have made the future situation any easier. With the signing of this treaty, the South Tyroleans have

been assured a certain standard of living and a degree of freedom, though of course they are aware that in the absence of good will, any treaty is just a scrap of paper. However, one advantage for our side is the pressure of public opinion on Italy. In any case, the treaty offers the following:

a mode of living is put in place; the continued existence of the South Tyroleans is assured, and all possibilities for future development remain intact;

if mutual understanding does not come about in South Tyrol, then intervention can subsequently be undertaken, and appeal can be made to an international forum; in any case, the treaty provides a point of departure.

Furthermore, he [Gruber] maintains that if the spirit in which this agreement was concluded prevails during subsequent negotiations, it will be possible to calm the situation down. Italy's path to re-establishing its position as a major power goes through Austria; therefore, it must strive to maintain cordial relations with Austria. He indicated throughout that Austria would be free to step in and work together with the parties if the South Tyroleans feel satisfied in Italy. This was frequently reiterated by Carandini.

The South Tyrol Question now has a basis. As weak as this may now be, it has nevertheless been internationally established; in any case, it now has come into existence legally, which previously was not the case.[62]

De Gasperi's signature revealed a piece of European mentality, or at least it seemed to do so at the time. Reality then turned out much differently: the Italians went on to renege on their commitments to the great disappointment of the South Tyroleans and the Austrians. They interpreted the agreement in extremely restrictive fashion, and that began with the implementation of autonomy. SVP representatives were now invited to Rome only for discussions about the formulation of the autonomy statute, but not for consultations about autonomy itself. As far as this was concerned, they were not even represented in the corresponding committee of the Constitutional Convention (the Province of Bozen was neither authorized to take part in the election of the delegates held on 6 July 1946, nor did it have a seat or a vote on the eighteen member constitutional committee for the region with special statutory status).

In a letter to De Gasperi dated 10 January 1948, Gruber informed the head of the Italian government that he had advised the SVP to accept the Trentino-Alto Adige Region under the proviso that the Italians accept the conditions of the minimum demands, but he made no effort to conceal his disappointment that, from the Viennese perspective, the decision that had been made did not uphold the spirit of the Paris Agreement. Nevertheless, on 18 January 1948, a South Tyrolean SVP delegation met with Italian envoy Silvio Innocenti. Over the following days, the South Tyroleans succeeded in making key improvements to the autonomy statute: the *Unterland* was returned to the Province of Bozen, and the province obtained legislative authority over cultural areas, was made a separate electoral district, and was granted administrative autonomy. On 28 January 1948, as a result of the concessions that had been made, South Tyrolean representatives Erich Amonn and Otto von Guggenberg wrote the now-notorious letter to Commission Chairman Tommaso Perassi, in which they stated that they regarded the establishment of the unitary region as the implementation of the Gruber-De Gasperi Agreement. Since then, the Italian Government has used this letter for propaganda purposes and as an expression of approval by the South Tyroleans of the Autonomy Statute of 1948.

Prior to this, extraordinarily difficult negotiations between Austria and Italy succeeded in producing an agreement for the re-acquisition of Italian citizenship by those who had opted to emigrate. This applied to about 150,000 South Tyroleans. They had opted for Germany in 1939. With their signature, they had lost their Italian citizenship but not yet received German citizenship because they had not left the country. Now they were displaced persons (DPs) in their own homeland, without any rights whatsoever. For absolutely everything official Italian permission was required: one could not get a job or even get married. As DPs, they had no right to vote. Therefore, Article 3 of the Paris Agreement was of particular importance.

The Italian government, however, took its own time in enacting the *Optantendekret*, waiting until the autonomy question had been resolved, and it did not take effect until 5 February 1948. Then they set up a special commission that took its time, and the delays continued.

VIII. 1948-1969: From Pseudo-Autonomy to the "Package"

"Break with Trient!"

It is no wonder that the entire process of dealing with the autonomy question gave rise to doubts among German-speaking South Tyroleans as to the transparency of Italian policymaking. This mistrust was thoroughly confirmed by events in the area of elementary education. In the fall of 1948, Italian schools were to be opened in Bozen, and instruction in a number of subjects was to be given in German. Under the headline "Danger is Imminent," the *Dolomiten* expressed the thoughts of the South Tyroleans:

> The Fascists, who still hold positions in the government, are not standing by idly. They are still striving to attain their goal, which is the same as it was twenty years ago – the gradual Italianization of South Tyrolean schools. Only their methods have changed. Brutal violence has been replaced by cunning, deception and evasion.

The protest by the SVP, however, particularly focused on the lack of implementation provisions regarding public housing construction. This was in the province's area of authority, so that criticism of the Italian government's residential construction policies was that much more intense. Just as in the establishment of a mixed-language school, the Italian government, through a massive public housing construction program and ongoing immigration, was making an effort to carry on the Fascists' policy of de-nationalization. For the German-speaking South Tyroleans, Italian immigration constituted the greatest danger. Thus, public housing construction took on a symbolic character to some extent, and it was precisely this problem that allowed the situation to subsequently escalate. In the 28 October 1953 issue of *Dolomiten*, Canon Michael Gamper wrote that 60,000 Italians had migrated to South Tyrol from 1946 to 1952. He added,

"What we South Tyroleans have been on since 1945 is a death march, unless relief arrives at the last minute."

In Gamper's opinion, Rome would not grant autonomy until the Italians were in the majority, and then the German-speakers would be powerless. The Italian press was reporting that immigration was attributable to economic forces, the dictates of which would be senseless to resist; furthermore, it would be unthinkable for a democratic country to try to prevent people from settling where they want. That was a spurious argument; indeed, the 60,000 figure cited by Gamper was not accurate either, but the "death march" image dominated the discussion from then on, for good reason: as newly-released Italian documents show, Rome was indeed pursuing a "51 percent" policy in South Tyrol, that is to say, ethnic infiltration.

Alcide De Gasperi resigned as prime minister in 1953, and times got even tougher. His successor, Giuseppe Pella, himself a former Fascist *Podestà*, invoked the right of self-determination to demand the return of Trieste to Italy while simultaneously denying the same right to the South Tyroleans. When, in 1954, Trieste actually was given back to Italy, this was not accompanied by more tolerant policies toward the South Tyroleans. The very opposite was the case. Political leaders, the police, and the legal machinery worked hand in hand to create an atmosphere of arrogant repression in South Tyrol.

One form of harassment followed the next. In March 1952, a law was passed that excluded South Tyrolean returning war veterans from preferential treatment that had been accorded them since 1948 in obtaining low-level public service jobs (such as rural letter carriers) in favor of Italian immigrants. Beginning in July 1952, all internal correspondence in government offices in South Tyrol had to be in Italian, even interactions between native German-speaking officials (such as school inspectors and principals). Prior to the parliamentary elections of 7 July 1953, the Neo-fascists (MSI), with the approval of the Christian Democrats, proposed a Communist as the joint Senate candidate of all Italians in South Tyrol to oppose the South Tyrolean ethnic group. Only the Communist's refusal to play along frustrated this plan! In April 1954, the Italian government rejected a kindergarten law that had been passed by the South Tyrolean provincial legislature because, although it did comply with the constitution, it nevertheless violated the relevant Fascist policy, not yet brought into conformity with the constitution's federal laws;

at the same time, it rejected a piece of nature preservation legislation because, while indeed in compliance with the relevant federal law, it was unconstitutional. On 20 June 1954, 5,000 South Tyrolean war invalids (including twelve men who were completely blind and 300 amputees, among them Silvius Magnago, who three years later became SVP chairman) marched silently through Bozen to protest the government's failure to pass pension legislation it had been promising for years. Several of the marchers were arrested.

In the fall of 1953, Fascist emergency legislation requiring military approval for transfers of real property, which had been suspended in 1947, was re-instituted in thirty-seven South Tyrolean communities. On 10 February 1955, judiciary officials in the province of Bozen circulated a memo from the Italian minister of justice pointing out that, on the basis of a Fascist ordinance dated 9 July 1939, it was forbidden to give children of Italian citizens foreign-language — that is, German — forenames. Legislation passed on 31 March 1955 reactivated the expropriation authority of the *Ente per le Tre Venezie* and provided it with a budget of 5 billion Lire; this body had been set up during the Fascist era for the "conquest of the land" in South Tyrol. In the very same month, the sizable *Brennerbad* real estate complex was confiscated on the basis of an 9 April 1939 expropriation decree that had not been carried out at the time. In April 1955, the Italian government made 2 billion Lire available for public housing construction (1.8 billion of which was earmarked for the City of Bozen). On 23 May 1955, two young South Tyroleans were sentenced to, respectively, twelve and sixteen months in prison for painting a barn with a slogan demanding the right of self-determination for South Tyrol.

In May 1957 came the changing of the guard within the South Tyrolean People's Party (SVP). The moderates were swept out of office; the "old men's" time had passed. At the SVP's Provincial Convention, fourteen new members were elected to the board of directors, and only six incumbents were reconfirmed. Silvius Magnago became the new party chairman and Friedl Volgger defeated Erich Amonn, the incumbent vice-chairman. The radical direction of the party thus also formally manifested itself within the uppermost leadership ranks.

This "palace revolution" meant a decisive turning point for the party and for South Tyrolean politics as a whole. The SVP's new top-level leadership was no longer prepared to carry on an intra-Italian dialogue; now, it believed that an uncompromising stance and straight talk to Trient and Rome — with its attention focused more strongly on Vienna and, above all, Innsbruck — was the way to achieve a better outcome for its ethnic constituency, and that meant at least provincial autonomy if not self-determination.

Sigmundskron Castle near Bozen, 17 November 1957: 35,000 South Tyroleans protest against pseudo-autonomy and call for a "Break with Trient!"

Escalation began in October 1957 when, within the framework of a 93 billion Lire national residential construction program, the Italian government budgeted 2.5 billion Lire for 5,000 dwellings in South Tyrol. On 17 November 1957, approximately 35,000 South Tyroleans gathered at Sigmundskron Castle. Their slogans were "Break with Trient!," "Protection from 48 Million," "South Tyrol Before the UN," and "Enough of the Pseudo-Autonomy." Aside from issues having to do with ethnic cultural policies, it was above all social welfare problems that led to the Sigmundskron rally. For example, there was dissatisfaction that only 7.1 percent of German-speaking South Tyroleans held public service jobs as compared to 52 percent of Italian speakers; of course, this was also a consequence of the Option, since it had been primarily the urban, German-speaking population that had emigrated.

What was publicly demonstrated at Sigmundskron is what had taken place in the SVP in May, and from this point on, the political winds grew stormier. In concert with Innsbruck and Vienna, a new phase began in South Tyrolean politics; for this reason as well, Sigmundskron has assumed very special significance in the history of South Tyrol. At the same time, Sigmundskron was a crucial test for new SVP Chairman Silvius Magnago, whose political ascent had just begun.

On 4 February 1958, immediately prior to the start of Austrian-Italian talks in Vienna, SVP representatives introduced a proposal for a constitutional law for South Tyrol in the Italian parliament. This bill maintained in "irrefutable fashion" that the Autonomy Statute of 1948, "which governs the fate of the German-speaking population of the region of autonomy," had "not put autonomy into operation" in actual practice. It was demanded that the Paris Agreement of 5 September 1946 finally be completely implemented by granting the territory of the province of Bozen and its population "true and actual autonomy"; this was said to be a just and rightful wish. Correspondingly, the province of Bozen was to be made an autonomous region with a special legal framework, and indeed one bearing a name in accordance with the history of this region and the language of the majority of its population, thus replacing the designation Alto Adige, a Napoleonic invention, whereby the memory of the Fascist ban on the use of the name South Tyrol would finally be eradicated. On 26 September 1958, the Provincial Legislature of Tyrol expressed support for this demand; this resolution went on to say that the legislature expected the Austrian federal government to press the Italian government to comply with this demand.

The Italian parliament, however, never debated this SVP bill (nor was any action taken in February 1959 when it was once again introduced into the Italian Chamber of Deputies by the South Tyrolean representatives after the crisis had broken out into the open). When, on 16 January 1959, the Italian government finally issued implementation regulations for public housing construction that removed practically all authority over this area that was still in the hands of the provincial government, the SVP, following prior consultation in Vienna, announced its resignation from the regional government. With this decision by the SVP, the region was paralyzed, and the situation took a critical turn.

Before the United Nations

With the signing of the State Treaty in 1955, Austria finally got back its independence and thus the freedom to act on its own in foreign policy matters as well. For the first time since 1945-46, South Tyrol became over the next several years one of the central issues of Austrian foreign policy as a result of massive pressure from Innsbruck. On 21 June 1955, Bruno Kreisky, the Socialist state secretary in the foreign office, made it clear what this would mean, namely, that "Austria, as a free and sovereign state, would now be in a better position to fulfill its obligations as laid out in the Treaty of Paris to look after the interests of the South Tyroleans *vis-à-vis* the government in Rome." A change of course was manifesting itself in Austria's South Tyrol policy. In 1956, Tyrolean Franz Gschnitzer, one of the most fervent advocates of the interests of South Tyrol, was named state secretary in the foreign office, and he saw to it that Chancellor Julius Raab took a more aggressive course. In July 1956, the chancellor accused Italy of not having complied with essential points of the Paris Agreement. This led to an exchange of memoranda between the two countries and subsequently to talks on the diplomatic level.

This exchange was initiated by the Austrian memorandum of 8 October 1956 that dealt with all open points of the Paris Agreement (such as the use of both languages to conduct official government business, the school system, filling public service positions, and so forth). It was suggested that a joint Italian-Austrian commission be set up to investigate these issues. The Italians answered in a note dated 30 January 1957, rejecting this proposal and re-iterating their view that they were in compliance with the Paris Agreement. A year later on 22 February 1958, the first exploratory talks between Vienna and Rome were held, whereby the Italian government expressly rejected the word "negotiations," since they denied Austria the right to negotiate the Paris Agreement, which they regarded as already having been fulfilled.

During the following months, these talks remained fruitless. The Italian government rejected the Austrian demand that provincial autonomy be granted to Bozen; at the same time, it adopted even stricter policies toward South Tyrol, which further exacerbated the ill will there toward Rome. These unproductive bilateral talks gave rise to the conviction in Innsbruck, Bozen, and Vienna that only by taking another approach would success be achieved. This approach meant to internationalize the South Tyrol problem — in other words, the UN (although, for a time, consideration was given to the International Court in The Hague).

The first step was taken by Foreign Minister Leopold Figl, who for years had done even less than Gruber for South Tyrol, and now, in light of the new situation, wanted to address this issue on the occasion of the tenth anniversary of the Council of Europe before its Consultative Assembly in Strasburg on 20 April 1959. Following intervention by Italian Delegate Roberto Lucifero and the Belgian chairman, though, he then skipped over the passage concerning South Tyrol in his address and demonstratively departed from Strasburg the next day.

At this time, neutral Austria had no friends among the Western powers when it came to the subject of South Tyrol; no one wanted unrest in the heart of Europe, to say nothing of a debate about minorities before the UN. The Western Allies advised against it and put pressure on the Austrian government. One of the many memoranda by the British ambassador in Rome, Ashley Clarke, explains the situation particularly well. On 28 February 1959, he wrote to Foreign Minister Selwyn Lloyd:

> At the time when the world lives under the threat of nuclear warfare and you yourself are engaged in difficult discussions with Mr. Krushchev, it may seem an anachronism that I should be addressing you on one of those minority questions which used to loom so large in the period between the two World Wars.

Furthermore, he gave the advice:

It would not, in my opinion, be to our interest to urge them [the Italians] to grant autonomy to South Tyrol. Despite what the Austrian ambassador said to me, I do not consider that it would settle the question. All the experience of the last years goes to show that the grant of autonomy would be followed by demands for a rectification of the frontier and a much more dangerous agitation would ensue, which would affect Italy's relations with Germany as well as with Austria. Such developments would not fail to have serious consequences for the future of the North Atlantic Alliance.[63]

At that time Italy, a member of the North Atlantic Treaty Organization (NATO), in a very clever move undercut Austrian aspirations to win the United States as mediator. As the first NATO government on the continent, they agreed to the deployment of U.S. nuclear missiles in Italy: the site would be South Tyrol. The State Department was pleased, and at the same time, South Tyrol was suddenly of strategic importance for the United States and NATO. From that moment, Italy could count on U.S. support in squelching any ideas of self-determination for South Tyrol. South Tyrol would never go back to neutral Austria.

Foreign Minister Bruno Kreisky elaborated on the South Tyrol problem for the first time before the UN on 21 September 1959. When talks in the State Department ended in disappointment, the Austrian government invited President Dwight Eisenhower in March 1960 to visit Austria. He would not come. In March, with hopes that John F. Kennedy would be elected president, he was approached for help. His answer showed some kind of understanding, but was non-committal.

In May 1960, Italian Prime Minister Fernando Tambroni suggested to Chancellor Julius Raab that secret talks be held in order to solve the South Tyrol problem in a more confidential setting after it became apparent that Austria definitely wanted to get this question onto the UN agenda. At this point, Kreisky was in favor of such talks, but the North and South Tyroleans were vehemently opposed. Kreisky was initially able to gain Raab's acceptance for his approach. Everything was prepared for secret talks to be held in Geneva, but then an intentional indiscretion occurred in Vienna, the

United States Senate
WASHINGTON, D.C.

March 28, 1960

Mr. Richard E. Sperber, Editor
Milwaukee Deutsche Zeitung
161 W. Wisconsin Ave.
Milwaukee, Wisconsin

Dear Mr. Sperber:

Thank you very much for your recent letter and for your kind words regarding my campaign. I was also interested to receive the article published in your newspaper.

I am aware of the deep interest which many members of the German-speaking community have in the question of South Tyrol. I am not aware that there will be a definite decision by the Austrian Government to present this matter to the United Nations. I understand that the Austrian Government had not yet determined that this is the best or most proper remedy for this long-standing issue.

I would, therefore, rather not comment upon a hypothetical event, but I can assure you that I shall give the matter my sympathetic attention if the United States Government is asked to render a verdict in the United Nations.

With kind regards and every good wish,

Sincerely yours,

John F. Kennedy

JFK/ml

Senator Kennedy's Correspondence regarding South Tyrol.

express purpose of which was to prevent these talks. As a result, they did not take place.

Instead, the Austrian government decided on 28 June 1960 to take the decisive step and to have the question placed on the agenda of the UN General Assembly. Three days before the Cabinet in Vienna took this decision, the British Foreign Minister Selwyn Lloyd had flown to Vienna to tell Kreisky:"Personally and as a friend I must say just this. I thought that there was nothing for him [Kreisky] personally in this action . . . and there was nothing in it for the South Tyroleans. It was a thoroughly dangerous operation which disturbed me."[64] The Austrian decision lent a new quality to the entire issue: the South Tyrol question had definitely become an international issue, and correspondingly international were the activities that led to the decision by the UN General Assembly. When Kreisky proposed the item "The Problem of the Austrian Minority in Italy" — without even mentioning the Paris Agreement — for inclusion in the UN's agenda, the government in Rome was up in arms and threatened to withdraw from the UN. Both parties then accepted the following British compromise: "The Status of the German-speaking Element in the Province of Bolzano (Bozen). Implementation of the Paris Agreement of 5 September 1946." After considering a number of drafts and at times heated discussions in one of the committees, the UN General Assembly on 31 October 1960 unanimously passed Resolution 1497/XV. This resolution confirmed Article 1 of the Paris Agreement as determinative for the purpose of the entire accord; this meant that also Article 2, which was to demarcate the frame of autonomy, ought to be "treated in a way that takes into consideration the ethnic character and the cultural and economic development of the South Tyroleans." The resolution called upon Italy and Austria to resume their negotiations in order to clear up all differences of opinion regarding the Paris Agreement and to settle their dispute. If, however, these negotiations failed to yield results within a reasonable amount of time, the resolution admonished both treaty signatories to make use of "peaceful means" provided for in the UN charter.

As was made quite clear in the resolution, the UN reaffirmed the legitimacy of Austria even having gotten involved in the South Tyrol issue, which Italy had called into question. The UN General

Assembly's decision was thus considered a success by the Austrian government.

In 1960 Austria takes the issue to the United Nations: Foreign Minister Bruno Kreisky makes his case. The General Assembly unanimously calls upon Italy and Austria to settle their dispute.

In accordance with the UN mandate, the Austrian and Italian foreign ministers met in January, May, and June 1961 in Milan, Klagenfurt, and Zurich. The negotiations were not productive. Italy declared that it was prepared only to implement more effectively the existing autonomy statute, but otherwise refused to make any amendments to its statutory regulations. For the Italian government, provincial autonomy for South Tyrol was absolutely out of the question! The negotiations in Zurich were broken off after one day without having accomplished anything. In light of Italy's uncompromising attitude, it is no wonder that the situation became increasingly aggravated over the course of 1961. There were already bombings being carried out in South Tyrol in January, February, and April; then in June came the "Night of Fire."

The Bombings

The subject of bombings remains a touchy subject to this day, especially in Tyrol, and this is even manifested by the term one uses to refer to those who carried them out. Depending on the particular point of view, they have been called freedom fighters, idealists, patriots, South Tyrolean activists, bomb throwers, terrorists, or all of these.

The bombings that are of interest in the context of this study occurred during the years from 1956 to 1969; in assessing them, one must carefully distinguish what happened, when, and how. The history of these bombings can be divided roughly into two phases. The first one lasted until about 1961, during which the watchword was to avoid endangering human life. The second phase continued to 1969; there were deaths, injuries and tremendous property damage. In the end, it was simply terrorism.

In September 1956, the first bombings targeted Fort Otto Huber, an army base in Bozen, and the railroad overpass near Siebeneich; they were carried out by South Tyroleans who were disappointed by the policies being pursued by the SVP leadership and who had organized a South Tyrolean Liberation Committee (*Befreiungsausschuss Südtirol*, or BAS). Their aim was self-determination for South Tyrol. More bombings took place in January 1957; in their aftermath, seventeen South Tyroleans were arrested. During the demonstration at Sigmundskron Castle in November 1957, BAS members clandestinely handed out fliers, the text of which had been written by the leading figure of the BAS, Sepp Kerschbaumer, "We want to remain German and not become slaves of a people that used treason and fraud to occupy our land without a fight and for forty years has been carrying on a system of exploitation and colonization that is worse than the methods the colonialists once used in Central Africa." Very soon, the South Tyroleans began to receive political, financial, and organizational support from sympathizers in Austria and Germany. Mention should be made first and foremost of the North Tyrolean journalist Wolfgang Pfaundler; Gerd Bacher, the editor-in-chief of the Vienna paper *Express* and later Austrian Broadcasting Company chairman; and Fritz Molden, then owner of Austria's largest news empire (*Die Presse, Die Abendpresse, Express, Wochenpresse*). In early 1959, Pfaundler had set up a BAS group in Innsbruck. A supporter who occupied a prominent political position was Aloys Oberhammer, a member of the North Tyrolean provincial government. When the foreign ministers' meeting in Milan on 27-28 January 1961 failed to produce results, demonstrative bombings of the symbols of Fascist repression occurred. The equestrian statue that stood before the Montecatini Works in Waidbruck, the "Aluminium Duce," was blown from its plinth into a thousand pieces. The second target was the house in Glen near Neumarkt where Ettore Tolomei had lived until his death in 1952. The explosive charge tore apart the balcony, ripped a two-meter-wide hole in the wall, and blew off half the roof. The message seemed to be clear: the South Tyroleans would not tolerate any further disregard of their rights.

The series of bombings reached its climax during the Sacred Heart of Jesus Festival on 11-12 June 1961. This night, which has gone down in the history of South Tyrol as the "Night of Fire," triggered a new wave of attacks. The "Night of Fire" bombings caused considerable property damage. Throughout the province, thirty-seven high-tension pylons were toppled, including nineteen in Bozen alone. Power transmission to northern Italian industrial plants was cut off, just as it was to the Bozen Industrial Zone. The bombings failed, however, to bring about a cool-down of the Bozen blast furnaces, which would have been a decisive blow. Nevertheless, the major power plants in Lana near Meran, in St. Anton, and in Sarntal were brought off-line, and others were damaged. While this series of bombings was being carried out, fliers calling for the right of self-determination for South Tyrol appeared.

11-12 June 1961: The "Night of Fire" in South Tyrol, with the bombing of 37 high-tension pylons.

Although in the wake of the bombings SVP leaders immediately distanced themselves from acts of violence, condemned them, and subsequently provided scant support to the men wanted for committing them, the bombings were later said by the perpetrators and their sympathizers to have been what triggered a change in Italy's South Tyrol policy. This is certainly not the case. At the suggestion of Minister of the Interior Mario Scelba, the Italian government — not because of but despite the bombings — appointed a commission consisting of eleven Italians and eight South Tyroleans; this "Commission of Nineteen", as it would come to be known, was assigned the task of examining the problem from all points of view and giving the government suggestions for a solution.

While this was going on in the summer of 1961, Scelba was turning South Tyrol into an armed camp; the land looked like it was on the brink of civil war. Immediately after the "Night of Fire," several hotels and inns were requisitioned in order to quarter troops and police. Searches were carried out in private homes on a daily basis, and within only a few days more than 150 South Tyrolean BAS men were arrested. Complaints of inhumane interrogation methods and brutal torture by the Italian police were common. The state's attorney in charge of the interrogations maintained that he had witnessed no mistreatment. The foreign press reported these charges; Silvius Magnago called for a rigorous investigation and punishment of the guilty policemen. Following the deaths of two South Tyroleans, parliamentary representatives from South Tyrol demanded the appointment of a board of inquiry, but the proposal was rejected. Meanwhile, the government of the Province of Tyrol vehemently appealed to Vienna, and demanded – successfully – that no legal proceedings having to do with South Tyrol be carried out in Austria as long as the corresponding proceedings in Italy had not been concluded.

On 20 August 1963, the trial of ten *carabinieri* accused of having mistreated South Tyrolean prisoners opened in Trient. Despite clear evidence having been presented, eight of them were found not guilty "due to proven innocence"; two were indeed found guilty, but these came under the terms of an amnesty that had been enacted in the meantime. The verdict elicited outrage particularly in South Tyrol and Austria, but in Germany as well; Austrian-Italian relations were approaching a nadir.

DEPARTMENT OF STATE

AIRGRAM

663.65/4-206

A-813   CONFIDENTIAL

TO : DEPARTMENT OF STATE   1962 APR 21 PM 12 59

INFO : Amconsul SALZBURG A-28
Amconsul VENICE A-64
Amembassy VIENNA A-51

RM/AN ANALYSIS & DISTRIBUTION BRANCH

FROM : Amembassy ROME   DATE: April 20, 1962

SUBJECT : SOUTH TYROL

REF :

Foreign Ministry is about to answer Austrian note of April 10 concerning future bilateral negotiations regarding Alto Adige (see Vienna despatch No. 915, April 12). According Benuzzi of Alto Adige Office, Italian reply will indicate that June would be acceptable time for resumption of talks and will add suggestion that meeting of Foreign Ministers be preceded by meeting at lower level to prepare ground. Italians expect work of Alto Adige Study Commission to be concluded by that time.

In this connection Benuzzi said Italians were perplexed at accounts of dissension within Commission which had appeared recently in Austrian papers (particularly Die Presse). Benuzzi said there had been no such disagreements within Commission and that topics on which differences of opinion were supposed to have been expressed were aspects of general subject of autonomy which Commission has not yet taken up. To Foreign Ministry these articles have appearance of propaganda attempt to impugn Commission's work, and they are wondering (1) whether Kreisky may be jealous of Commission for possibility that it may produce steps toward resolution of Alto Adige problem independently of Austrian Government, and (2) whether Austrians may not actually wish to keep South Tyrol issue alive until elections next autumn, so that activities of Austrian Government in this matter may be used as helpful talking point in election campaign. However, it was also evident from other remarks made by Benuzzi during same conversation that Italians had noted more reasonable attitude exemplified by fact that Austrians had recently arrested prominent terrorists, that they had cooperated with Swiss in search for others, and that two officials had explicitly stated in recent speeches that Berg Isel Bund fomented terrorism.

REINHARDT
JWA

CONFIDENTIAL

PCZ:JWAuchincloss:jal 4/19/62

The State Department is well-informed about the situation.

On 9 December 1963 in Milan, the first South Tyrolean bombing trial began with ninety-four defendants, of whom sixty-eight were then in custody. The accused were charged with ninety-two bombings of high-tension pylons, and eight bombings of apartment buildings under construction as well as bombings of military installations and collective charges of murder (Giovanni Postal, an Italian street maintenance employee, had been killed while handling explosives) and, finally, the charge of high treason. The verdicts came on 16 July 1964: four of the defendants still at large each got over twenty years in prison, eight were sentenced to terms between ten and twenty years, thirty-five defendants got between four and ten years, and twenty-seven were found not guilty or were amnestied; forty-six South Tyroleans were released from prison, and twenty-two remained in custody. Half a year later, Sepp Kerschbaumer died in the penitentiary in Verona; 15,000 South Tyroleans joined his funeral cortege. (Only South Tyroleans actually went to prison, not one "intellectual" North Tyrolean ever saw a prison cell from within.)

The bottom line of the Milan verdict was that Judge Gustavo Simonetti dismissed the charges filed against the defendants by the state's attorney based on Article 241 (offense against the unity of the state) and Article 283 (offense against the constitution) of the Italian criminal code — punishable by life imprisonment — and thus reached a verdict on the basis of other crimes (illegal possession of weapons and explosives, damage to property, and so forth). This had been made possible by the defendants having accepted their attorneys' strategy and testified that their objective had been autonomy and not self-determination. The quite "mild" verdicts, which were the result of intervention by the Italian government, were also acknowledged and applauded by the SVP and Austria as a token of good will in the midst of a tense political atmosphere. Many of the convicted South Tyroleans were later granted early release from prison.

Beginning in 1962-63, the actions became more radical. The principle of avoiding endangerment of human life was no longer observed. From this point on, it was Austrian and German citizens who were increasingly involved in committing acts of terrorism. Then, the Italians succeeded in planting agents in the group led by the South Tyroleans Georg Klotz and Luis Amplatz. Both had been convicted at the Milan bombing trial *in absentia* since they had fled to North Tyrol. On 7 September 1964, Luis Amplatz was shot dead in a barn near Saltaus in Passeiertal in South Tyrol, and Georg Klotz was gravely wounded by an agent working for the Italian intelligence agency: Christian Kerbler, a Tyrolean.

South Tyrol now became an arena for spy agencies foreign and domestic, neo-Nazi groups and pan-German circles. This initiated a phase (1965-67) in which the attacks reached a crescendo of brutality and unscrupulousness, and claimed a total of fourteen lives. In return, Italians were carrying out attacks in Austria that resulted in deaths. This terror was, in any case, absolutely counterproductive for the autonomy negotiations. At the second Milan bombing trial held in 1966, long prison terms were again handed down against numerous defendants in absentia. Italy then accused Austria of complicity with the terrorists, and in June 1967 used its veto to block Austria's negotiations with the European Economic Community (EEC).

The assumption in Vienna — which events would prove well-founded in short order — was that Italy's EEC veto had opened up a completely new diplomatic front that would be a source of conflict for some time to come. On 11 July 1967, Lujo Tončić-Sorinj, Kreisky's successor as foreign minister, submitted a report to the Council of Ministers that critically summarized the overall situation. He began by acknowledging that relations between Austria and Italy in the wake of the incidents on 25 June — four dead as the result of the bombing in a place called Porzescharte — had reached "their lowest point since 1945." Certain Italian circles that were said to have long been unfavorably disposed to an agreement being reached between Austria and Italy on the South Tyrol question were fully exploiting the situation by exacerbating the tangible and genuine tensions that did exist. The aim of this circle, in which Tončić included Italian Foreign Minister Amintore Fanfani, was "to force Austria out of the bilateral negotiations that had been going on for more than ten years; thereafter, if they would undertake any effort at all to solve the South Tyrol problem, then unilaterally through purely internal measures that would no longer be subject to any oversight whatsoever by Austria."

Italy simultaneously demanded that Austria revise its criminal code and made it clear during secret bilateral talks in London that without new efforts by Vienna to bring about "effective and spectacular" progress in combating terror, there would neither be an agreement on the South Tyrol question nor a lifting of Italy's EEC veto.

The "Package"

Following the unproductive talks in Milan, Klagenfurt, and Zurich (January, May, and June 1961), Austria once again brought the South Tyrol question before the UN General Assembly, which on 28 November 1961 renewed its resolution from the previous year. In the meantime, the Commission of Nineteen had gotten down to business, holding its first session on 21 September 1961. It completed its work with the submission of a final report to Prime Minister Aldo Moro on 10 April 1964. Three months of work had been planned; in fact, consultations lasted almost three years.

The Commission of Nineteen was set up first and foremost with the intention of forcing Austria out of the "South Tyrol business" and enabling the Italians to settle things on their own. At least this was to have been the argument presented at the UN in the fall of 1961, and it was indeed utilized quite effectively by the Italians. However, as is so often the case with committees, the Commission of Nineteen developed a momentum and a life of its own thanks to its chairman, well-to-do Socialist Paolo Rossi. The bilateral talks between Rome and Vienna had reached a dead end; thus, increasing attention was focused on the work of this commission, and its results were awaited with a great sense of anticipation. In South Tyrol itself, the Italians — and especially the *carabinieri* — continued to lord it over the locals.

The results of the Commission's work already came to be referred to as the "Package," and they constituted the core of what was officially accepted as the "Package" in 1969 by the SVP's provincial convention. By this point, separate autonomy for the province of South Tyrol as called for by the SVP and the government in Vienna was a long-forgotten topic. The aim of the measures that made up this Package was undermining regional autonomy.

The undisputable fact is that it was the new center-left government under Aldo Moro and Giuseppe Saragat, which had some understanding for minorities, that opened the possibility for constructive discussions and not the bombings or the terror. On 16 December 1964, only one year after this government had been formed, the two Socialist foreign ministers, Bruno Kreisky and Giuseppe Saragat (who, like Kreisky, had lived in exile; his daughter had been born in Vienna), reached a basic agreement at a secret conference held in Paris. On 8 January in Innsbruck, Kreisky delivered a report on the results of those negotiations to representatives of North and South Tyrol and recommended they accept the deal. The representatives refused because the SVP insisted on further concessions in the areas of commerce, industry, finance, and labor. The proposal provided for only a short-term internationalization, which of course brought with it the disadvantage that, following Austrian recognition, the implementation of the Package would have become an internal affair of Italy. This was too little for the North Tyroleans. The North and South Tyroleans had already agreed to reject the deal a few days before when they conferred among themselves. This soured Kreisky on the South Tyrol question. At the same time, he also rejected any other solution. Furthermore, once the People's Party (*Österreichische Volkspartei*, or ÖVP) could form a solo government without the need of a coalition partner in the spring of 1966, he and the Socialist Party (*Sozialistische Partei Österreichs*, or SPÖ) followed a course of total opposition to the solution being pursued by his successor, and he even made an effort to create a split within the ranks of the SVP.

The new Austrian Foreign Minister, Lujo Tonĉić-Sorinj, began direct talks with Italian Foreign Minister Amintore Fanfani in 1966. Italy now began to propose an "all-inclusive offer," and the Package debuted at the end of August 1966. On 1 September, an SVP committee approved the results of the talks and recommended that the provincial convention accept them after certain "clarifications," which Magnago was expected to be able to take care of with Prime Minister Aldo Moro.

What still remained open was the problem of "effectively anchoring the Package internationally," which the SVP committee forcefully demanded in March 1967. The negotiations in this area were drawn out over three years, during which absolute secrecy was maintained. They have to be seen in the context of the uneasy political situation in 1967 and 1968: the previously mentioned bombings and the Italian EEC veto, as well as parliamentary elections and governmental crises in Italy that served above all as a way for the opponents of the Package to postpone a decision over and over again.

Popular politicians at the time (from left to right): Tyrol's Governor Bruno Wallnöfer, Austria's Chancellor Josef Klaus, South Tyrol's long time Governor Silvius Magnago, Austria's Foreign Minister Lujo Tončić-Sorinj.

As far as anchoring the accord on an international basis was concerned, Italy had proposed an arbitration tribunal in 1964. Now, it suddenly withdrew this proposal and rejected any treaty-like agreements in connection with the Package. Thus, all that remained was an offer to anchor the accord politically. This was referred to as the "operations calendar," which was meant to be a timetable specifying deadlines for the implementation of the Package, at the end of which Austria was to declare an end to the dispute. Foreign Ministers Pietro Nenni and Kurt Waldheim agreed on this operations calendar at a meeting of the Ministers' Committee of the member states of the Council of Europe on 13 May 1969. The measures were designed to go hand in hand with steps taken by Austria like the meshing of two cogwheels, or, as Kurt Waldheim once put it: "The Package is the train; the operations calendar is the timetable." Thereafter, Italy would withdraw its EEC veto.

Copenhagen, November 1969: the Foreign Ministers of Austria, Kurt Waldheim (left) and Italy, Aldo Moro, agree on the autonomy solution for South Tyrol.

The SVP provincial convention constituted one last hurdle, but the Austrian government did not want to act without its approval. In October 1969, the SVP's executive board decided by a vote of forty-one to twenty-three to recommend the acceptance of the Package and the operations calendar to the provincial convention. At 9:30 a.m. on 22 November 1969, this special convention of the SVP began in the main assembly hall of the *Kurhaus* in Meran, where 1,111 delegates from the seven electoral districts of Bozen, Brixen, Meran, Pustertal, Sterzing, Unterland, and Vinschgau gathered. Opponents and advocates of the Package faced off, and the "battle" began. On one side stood the proponents headed by Governor Silvius Magnago, Friedl Volgger, and Members of Parliament (MPs) Roland Riz and Karl Mitterdorfer; across from them were the opponents of the Package, including Senator Peter Brugger, Vice-Governor Alfons Benedikter and *Landesrat* Joachim Dalsass.

Early in the morning of the next day, after an eighteen-hour debate, the Package was approved by the narrow margin of 583 to 492 (or 52.8 percent to 44.6 percent). Then, on 30 November, Moro and Waldheim met in Copenhagen to set up a concrete schedule for the Package and the operations calendar. The task they faced, as their communiqué put it, was to end the current dispute between Austria and Italy.

The next day, 1 December, Chancellor Josef Klaus delivered a statement on the subject of "terrorism" before the Austrian Parliament, including the following passage:

> In previous years, acts of violence have been committed by certain irresponsible individuals in connection with the South Tyrol problem. We deeply regret that this has led to the loss of human lives and property damage. I hereby repeat most emphatically that we condemn the use of violence as a means to attain political goals.

Seven days later, on 8 December, Italy withdrew its veto at the EEC Ministers' Council meeting in Brussels. On 2 December, the treaty had been initialled at the International Court in Vienna; on 3 December, Prime Minister Mariano Rumor announced the measures for South Tyrol before the Italian Parliament. In the subsequent vote, 269 representatives were for and twenty-six against Rumor's declaration, with eighty-eight abstaining.

On 15 December 1969, Chancellor Klaus delivered a corresponding declaration before the Austrian Parliament, where the vote of approval was far from a landslide. As expected, the socialist SPÖ made a motion whereby the entire Package — and not only the Treaty of Paris — would be submitted to the International Court for its scrutiny. This motion was defeated the next day by eighty-three ÖVP votes against seventy-nine from the opposition (seventy-three SPÖ, 6 FPÖ — the Liberals or *Freiheitliche Partei Österreichs*). The government's declaration as delivered by Klaus then passed by the same margin, and the government was thus given the go-ahead to proceed in accordance with the operations calendar.

This Package actually amounted to nothing more than the sum of Italy's concessions to expand South Tyrolean autonomy that had not adequately been provided for by the Autonomy Statute of 1948. It contained 137 so-called "measures" affecting the population of South Tyrol, the enactment of ninety-seven of which required amendment to the Autonomy Statute of 1948 (by means of constitutional law), eight with implementation regulations to be appended to that autonomy statute, fifteen with simple federal laws, nine with administrative orders, and the remainder with administrative acts. The most important part of the Package was the amendment of the old autonomy statute, or rather the approval of a new statute, which then took place with the passage of Constitutional Law Nr. 1 dated 10 November 1971 (and which took effect on 20 January 1972). Measure 137 provided for the appointment of a standing commission to deal with the problems of the province of Bozen. Once the Package had been fulfilled, Austria committed itself to filing a declaration with the UN that the dispute had been resolved (points thirteen through eighteen of the operations calendar).

What were the chief differences between the old autonomy statute and the new one? In the headline of the very first section, mention is no longer made of a "Tyrolean Etschland"; rather, the name "South Tyrol" is used. In the first chapter, the following was added to Article 3: "Autonomy of a special type and including certain particular provisions is granted to the provinces of Trient and Bozen on the basis of this statute." This short sentence expressed what was to be brought to fruition in the new autonomy statute. All of Italy is divided into regions, and these in turn are divided into provinces, whose authority in various areas has been precisely delineated over the course of the constitutionally mandated process of decentralization. In numerous instances, however, the region had the final say-so, which, in the case of the "Trentino-Tiroler Etschland" meant that power was in the hands of the Italian majority, which exercised it to the disadvantage of the South Tyroleans. This had, of course, been the problem since 1948.

For the protection of the German-speaking minority — which, however, constituted a majority in the Province of Bozen — a statute that was unprecedented in Italy had now been worked out. Indeed, its provisions left the region in its previous dimensions intact; nevertheless, most of the areas over which the region had power were now under the authority of the two provinces. For South Tyrol, this meant that it was in the hands of its German-speaking majority "for the protection and preservation of its ethnic and cultural uniqueness" as a minority within the Italian state.

The second and third chapters listed the respective areas of authority of the region and the two provinces, which made it clear that the new autonomy statute would transfer numerous areas of authority from the region to the two autonomous provinces. The most important of these were subsidized residential construction, hunting and fishing, parks for the protection of endangered plants and animals, streets, water supply, sewage system and public works, communication and transportation systems, the takeover of public services, tourism and the hospitality industry, agriculture and forestry, hydraulic engineering, public welfare, and the construction of kindergartens and schools.

Furthermore, the Ladins, who had been accorded almost no consideration by the Autonomy Statute of 1948, were mentioned at length, particularly in Article 19 that dealt with the school problem: "The Ladin language will be used in the kindergartens and taught in the primary schools in Ladin villages." In Article 102, these rights were extended to include the Ladins in the province of Trient.

It is also worth mentioning that instruction in the respective second language was now made mandatory beginning in the second or third grade in primary schools and in secondary schools, an extraordinarily important precondition for achieving the goal of making the entire population of South Tyrol bilingual (Article 19). Furthermore, the provincial government agencies set up expressly for this purpose were accorded tremendous latitude in "approving, setting down, and promulgating laws and ordinances." These forms of authority were divided into primary and secondary levels of responsibility (Articles 4 and 5). "Primary" meant that the province could enact laws and set standards, though without violating the constitution and the fundamental principles of Italian jurisprudence, the country's international commitments, and the basic guidelines of the economic and social reforms of the Italian state. "Secondary" expanded these limitations further to include the basic principles established in federal laws. This course — shifting more authority from the region to the provinces — was pursued throughout the entire autonomy statute. This statute constituted legally established guidelines that, on the basis of implementation regulations incorporated into the Package, would take on legal validity and be enforced.

IX. From the "Package" to the Present

The operations calendar accompanying the Package stipulated that all measures were to be in place by 20 January 1974, or their implementation was to have commenced by then. Thus, there was growing anticipation to find out which group of participants in the SVP provincial assembly in November 1969 would prove to have been right: the opponents or the proponents of the Package, the skeptics or the pragmatists. Developments got off to a good start. On 16 December 1969, the Italian government gave the go-ahead to begin work on the new autonomy statute to the Commission of Nine that had been set up for this purpose. This body, composed of South Tyrolean and Italian representatives, then prepared the statute and the revisions of the simple federal laws. The new autonomy statute went into law on 20 January 1972. In comparison to the first statute from 1948 and to those of the other Italian regions, this represented real progress for South Tyrol. The land was now once again officially "South Tyrol," and there was the "Autonomous Province of Bozen-South Tyrol." In accordance with Articles 8 and 9, several primary and secondary areas of authority that had previously come under the purview of the region or the state were transferred to South Tyrol. Among the most important of these was authority over the schools and tourism. A few months later, the parliament in Rome passed an omnibus law including thirteen Package measures. Measures 106 to 120 dealt with community secretaries, the reintroduction of German names, the dissolution of the *Ente nazionale per le Tre Venezie*, and the assignment of various responsibilities within the province of Bozen.

A Commission of Twelve was set up to work out the Package measures. This was composed of six representatives each from the state and the region; of the latter, the Bozen and Trient provincial assemblies and the Regional Council each sent two representatives. At least half of these six members had to be German-speaking. In addition, a subcommission — the Commission of Six — was formed to work out the implementation regulations having to do exclusively with the province of Bozen.

The implementation regulations were decreed by the Italian government, though the various commissions had a right of a "hearing." Thus, delays in implementing the Package during the 1970s were attributable to "the experts being overloaded with work and the negotiations being interrupted as a result of frequent government crises," as well as to the fact that the SVP wanted to get every possible advantage out of the statute and therefore was not always in any particular hurry to wrap things up. Nevertheless, there were decisive breakthroughs in two areas: schools and the *Proporz* system.

The Commission of Six worked out the school measures in early 1973. According to these implementation regulations, the province took over the administration of almost all aspects of the school system. The measures also guaranteed that pupils would receive instruction in their mother tongue; therefore, the teachers had to be fluent in that language. This rule applied to all three language groups. An additional point had to do with bilingualism. All pupils were to begin learning their respective second language in the second or third grade. This new autonomy was a milestone for South Tyrol's schools.

In 1976, one of the most important measures for the protection of the South Tyroleans was enacted — the "*Proporz* Decree" that went into law on 30 November.

Thirty years after the signing of the Gruber-De Gasperi Agreement, a start would finally be made in implementing the fundamental principle of an "appropriate" policy of filling public service positions (in the government bureaucracy and semi-official areas) as expressed in Article 1 of that accord. Only those who are familiar with the history of South Tyrol during the time of Fascism as well as after 1945 can truly appreciate the significance of this measure. In those days, the South Tyroleans were almost totally excluded from public service jobs. Now, a corrective had finally been put in place. The *Proporz* Decree was designed to assure that positions would be allocated to members of all three language groups based on their relative numerical strength; the precondition for this was adequate knowledge of the Italian and German languages. The certificate of bilingualism, the *Patentino*, was the indispensable "ticket" for admission to the civil service — and subsequently became one of the most hated of all official documents, particularly by the Italians.

On the whole, little progress was made in implementing the Package up through the end of the 1970s. The general mood in the province deteriorated among German-speaking South Tyroleans, and especially among the Italians, who feared losing the dominant position they had enjoyed until then. Moreover, they objected to the growing prosperity of the South Tyroleans, who were totally dominant in their bailiwicks of tourism and agriculture. In addition, they had little opportunity for social and economic mobility. In the province as a whole, they were a linguistic minority. Most of them lived in Bozen, which prevented the dismantling of cultural barriers and underscored the relative weakness and isolation of the Italians — with the exception of those in Bozen.

There were problems with the government in Rome. In the early 1980s, numerous bills that had been hammered out by the South Tyrolean legislature and sent to Rome for review were rejected and referred back to Bozen. This happened when the legislature had exceeded its authority, or if Rome maintained that it had done so. The legislature could, indeed, repeatedly resubmit a rejected bill, but the government could likewise keep referring it back. Then, the matter was left up to the Constitutional Court, which could often take a year to reach a decision. This put the provincial legislature under pressure "to display its eager compliance with the express preferences" of the government.

The SVP got another taste of Rome's "bad mood" in the matter of granting equal status to the German language. The time had finally come to put an end to the absurd situation whereby German-speaking South Tyroleans could be interrogated by the police in what for them was a foreign language. In courts of law as well, trials were at last to be held in the defendant's mother tongue. What was missing, though, was above all the necessary infrastructure. "Translators and interpreters, necessary to guarantee a minimum level of bilingualism, are practically nonexistent. The only ones available to perform this service are low-paid temps with scant qualifications," the South Tyrolean weekly magazine *FF* complained in 1984.

Italian lawyers who feared a loss of income were particularly ill disposed to the SVP demands. One alternative — namely, learning

German — was for them an imposition that could well be demanded of street sweepers but not of attorneys. In turn, the SVP wanted nothing to do with the Italian parties' proposal to conduct all trials bilingually. Indeed, this would have doubled the duration of trials, although that certainly would have accommodated those who had an interest in slowing the wheels of justice.

On 5 December 1986, the parliament in Rome began a South Tyrol debate, which ended in February 1987 with the approval of two resolutions. In them, the government committed itself to enacting within that same year the still-outstanding implementation regulations as part of an all-encompassing solution. There had been no prior consultation with the SVP, which then also condemned this mode of proceeding as "a grave violation of the Package, the autonomy statute, international commitments, and the agreements that had been arrived at between the representatives of the majority parties in the South Tyrolean legislature."

The "autonomy climate" deteriorated markedly over the ensuing months. The number of rejected bills rose. In 1987, regions with special statutory status had a rejection rate of 22 percent; in those with normal statutory status, it was 29 percent; in South Tyrol, the rate was 44.2 percent with the trend rising in comparison to previous years (in 1984, 10 percent; in 1985, 38.5 percent; in 1986, 29.7 percent). In late 1987, Silvius Magnago stated in an interview that the government in Rome initially used delaying tactics instead of having done everything possible "to work together with us to bring about passage of the still-outstanding implementation regulations." Meanwhile, the bombings were still going on, carried out by a few radical groups like One Tyrol.

On 9 November 1989, just as the Berlin Wall was coming down, that portion of the implementation regulations took effect that has to do with the equal status of the German and Italian languages in citizens' dealings with the government administration as well as the use of Ladin in the conduct of official business. There would still be a bit of a wait for bilingualism in the court system and law enforcement.

On 15 November, the Chamber of Deputies in Rome agreed on measures to revamp the finances of the Province of South Tyrol; that is, the financial relations between the state, the region, and both autonomous provinces of Bozen and Trient were overhauled. This law took effect on 4 December 1989, although certain details were still to be brought into conformity with the implementation regulations. The objective of this revision was to insure sufficient income for the provinces of Trentino and South Tyrol as well as for the region based on the tax revenues generated within their respective territories.

Almost simultaneously, Italy's head of government Giulio Andreotti raised the prospect of the final passage of the Package taking place before the end of 1990, and similarly optimistic statements also came from Foreign Minister Gianni de Michelis. But, as had happened so often before, new difficulties in the Italian Parliament delayed the final passage of precisely those legal measures that were indispensable for putting the complete Package into place, such as the redrawing of the senate electoral districts, setting up separate branches of the province's supreme court, and establishing a branch of the Trient juvenile court in Bozen.

On 30 November, the Council of Ministers in Rome finalized new implementation regulations for the railroad, whereby, in accordance with the verdict of the Supreme Court, the railroad administration was mandated to observe a hiring policy in South Tyrol that complied with the *Proporz* and bilingualism rules then in effect.

Finally, on 27 April 1991 the "changing of the guard" took place in South Tyrol. Silvius Magnago, who, after twenty-eight years as governor, had turned over the office to Luis Durnwalder on 17 March 1989, decided against running again for party chairman, the post he had held since 1957. He was succeeded on that day by Roland Riz, the governor's long-time political associate who had extensive experience as an MP in Rome. During the final phase of the Package negotiations, the watchwords of the SVP were "march separately and strike together." The new SVP chairman imparted fresh impetus to the negotiations; he wanted to wrap up the Package speedily, and he thus put massive pressure on Rome to work out a quick solution to the questions that were still open.

Critics and skeptics pointed to the ongoing efforts to undermine autonomy by central government officials in Rome, the debate of fundamental constitutional reform in Italy, as well as the self-determination discussion that had flared up anew in South Tyrol and had led to a rally on 15 September 1991 on the Brenner that was given intense coverage in the media. "Break with Rome! — United

Province Now" was the motto of this event. On 26 September, Riz presented an eight-point program to get things moving forward. It combined familiar SVP platform points, such as the call for redrawing the senatorial electoral districts in the Trentino-South Tyrol region and setting up a Bozen branch of the Trient provincial supreme court, with new demands for the "amplification and amendment of open implementation regulations, and the repeal of those measures that, in the meantime, have undermined our autonomy," as well as "establishing the actionability and the international recognition of our autonomy not only in Rome but in Brussels as well." Academic degrees earned in Austria should also be made valid retroactively.

What was new and important about all this was the clear signal it delivered to Rome that Riz characterized the acceptance of these points as a *conditio sine qua non* for the SVP's consent to Austria filing a declaration with the UN that the conflict had been resolved. Riz also set a kind of deadline for compliance with his demands: 23 November 1991, when the SVP's province-wide convention would take place. Surely, Riz also realized that it would be impossible to come up with a solution to the questions that were still open in such a short time, but his aim was twofold: to spur the Commissions of Six and Twelve to intensify their work, and to break out of the state of stagnation that had set in on the legal measures that effected South Tyrol.

On 10 October 1991, the Chamber of Deputies in Rome passed a bill providing for setting up a branch of the province supreme court and of the Trient juvenile court in Bozen. In order to pass this law, the government had to repeatedly ask for a vote of confidence. The resistance toward this measure crossed all party lines, which, among other consequences, had led the judiciary committee responsible for this bill to file a series of expert reports calling for its rejection.

The SVP convention on 23 November 1991 was another one of those stormy sessions the party was experiencing so often in those days. Should they agree to approve the Package, or wait until all points were definitively finalized? The pragmatists in the SVP's top ranks proceeded dexterously. Riz accepted the demand that Italy and Austria could agree to a declaration of conflict resolution only when the state of autonomy at the time the Package was finalized was in complete agreement with both the content and the spirit of the 1969

Package; he decisively rejected a second proposal whereby, prior to approving the Package, all points that were still open had to be fulfilled and all areas of authority that had been undermined since 1969 had to be restored. In the show-down vote, the majority of the delegates went along with Riz. No small contribution to this was the influence exerted by Honorary Chairman Silvius Magnago, who brought his entire prestige and power of persuasion to bear. Also rejected was a proposal to have Austria scrutinize the compromise having to do with the Alignment and Coordination Authority that had been worked out between the SVP and the government in Rome. On the other hand, the convention adopted the resolution proposed by Riz whereby "the restoration of the rights and privileges that had been undermined since 1988 would not be made a condition for the finalization of the Package, and there would be no insistence on fulfillment down to the last detail of the measures promised in 1969."

The day of 18 December 1991 finally brought implementation of the Package's Measure 111; that is, the senate in Rome passed the bill providing for redrawing the senatorial election districts in South Tyrol. There would henceforth be three districts, and thus three senate seats.

In the meantime, party Chairman Riz had obtained assurance from Prime Minister Andreotti that his summary report compiled at the conclusion of the current legislative period would refer to the measures enacted by parliament and the government since 1969 for the benefit of the South Tyrolean population, and would establish a direct connection to the Treaty of Paris, i.e. the Gruber-De Gasperi Agreement. The text of this programmatic statement would be passed along to Austria with the wish that it regard this as an adequate guarantee that the Package measures were solidly established in international law. In his farewell address before parliament on 30 January 1992, Andreotti declared that the Package had been fulfilled. The Italian government was said to have lived up to its obligations in implementing the 1969 Package, and future changes could be undertaken with the approval of the South Tyrolean population, but there was no sign of the promised reference to the Treaty of Paris and thus no linkage to the Package measures and establishment of them in international law.

Then, on 22 April 1992, Bruno Bottai, the general secretary of the

Italian Foreign Ministry, turned over to Austrian Ambassador Emil Stafflmayr the now-famous note together with a list of the implementation orders for the measures passed by the Italian government and the Italian Parliament for the benefit of South Tyrol — with explicit reference to the Treaty of Paris. It stated that, due to its "practical relevance," the special statute for the Trentino-South Tyrol region was being enclosed as well, legislation "which, over the course of establishing the institutional framework of the Autonomous Province of Bozen, aimed to implement the broadest possible autonomy and to assure the protection of the German-speaking minority as mandated by the Treaty of Paris, which, among its many provisions, calls for guaranteeing an autonomous process of passing and enforcing laws."

With the handing over of this note, the fifty-day term set out in the operations calendar of 1969 during which Austria was to deliver a declaration of conflict resolution before the UN began to run. The connection that the note established between the realization of South Tyrolean autonomy and the objective of protecting ethnic minorities as this has also emerged within the framework of the Conference on Security and Cooperation in Europe (CSCE) as well as the reference to the Treaty of Paris were, on the other hand, interpreted as constituting a step in the direction of complying with the SVP's desire that autonomy be solidly anchored internationally and that it be actionable before appropriate international legal authorities.

In a secret ballot conducted at a special SVP convention on 30 May 1992, 82.6 percent of the delegates voted for delivering a declaration of conflict resolution. The government of the Province of Tyrol did the same on 1 June, followed by the Tyrolean Provincial Assembly on 4 June, and, after a five-and-a-half-hour discussion on 5 June in Vienna, the Austrian Parliament by an overwhelming majority (125 "ayes" from the SPÖ, ÖVP and the Greens; 30 "nays" from the FPÖ). During the debate, both Chancellor Franz Vranitzky and Foreign Minister Alois Mock reaffirmed Austria's commitment to fulfilling its role as protector in the future, including appeal to the International Court if necessary.

These guidelines were integrated into a resolution adopted by parliament — the wording of which was communicated along with the declaration of conflict resolution by means of a verbal note from the Austrian foreign minister to the Italian ambassador in Austria —

as was the reaffirmation of the position that the Treaty of Paris did not constitute relinquishment of South Tyrol's right of self-determination and that the measures aimed at fulfilling the Package were, so to speak, the implementing act of the Treaty of Paris. Once the Austrian government composed its declaration of conflict resolution on 11 June, it was time to take the final step on 19 June 1992: there, at the UN, where in 1960 Austria and Italy had been called upon to resolve their differences, this dispute was formally ended. The Austrian and Italian ambassadors to the UN handed over the "Notification of the Termination of Conflict" to UN Secretary General Boutros Boutros-Ghali.

In accepting the notification document, Boutros-Ghali underscored the significance of this step and called this mode of resolving a minority dispute between two states exemplary. At the CSCE successor conference in Helsinki in July 1992, Italian Foreign Minister Vincenzo Scotti also pointed with pride to the resolution of the conflict between Austria and Italy, a solution that might also serve as a model for the protection of minorities within the framework of the CSCE.

Conclusion

Since 1918, South Tyrol has been under foreign rule. It has been a rule by those who only during the last thirty years have been prepared to pursue a minority policy that even comes close to deserving the term. The new "masters" of the house did not like the former owners, the South Tyroleans. Nobody knows what would have happened if Fascism had not come to Italy. But it did, and it brought to South Tyrol a merciless denationalization policy designed to devastate the South Tyroleans. That goal was never really achieved, although the majorification policy pursued since 1935, with its massive immigration of Italians, certainly would have produced fundamental changes there over the long run. The former "German" Bozen with now roughly 75 percent Italians is a good example for that.

The most crushing blow to South Tyrol, however, was delivered not by the Fascists, but by the National Socialists – by Hitler and his agents. That approximately 86 percent of the South Tyroleans would vote for resettlement indicates how effective Nazi propaganda really was in the area, helped along as it was by continued Italian harassment, and by rumors that those who stayed would be shipped to Sicily, or worse. The lack of solidarity among South Tyroleans in this crisis, and afterwards, with the resettlers being denounced as "deserters" and "traitors to their land" while they themselves came to treat those who stayed like lepers, is one of the nastiest and saddest chapters in the history of South Tyrol.

The years after 1945 witnessed an almost identical repetition of what transpired after 1918-19. Hopes were dashed as before, and there was no return to Austria. The Allies had no interest in revising the Brenner border. There was no plebiscite and no self-determination, as South Tyrol became the first victim of the emerging Cold War.

The South Tyroleans and their supporters stood empty-handed in Vienna, Innsbruck, and Bozen in the summer of 1946. In the end there was only the Gruber-De Gasperi Agreement, and without the massive pressure exerted by the British upon the Italians, it might not even have come to that. Would that have been better in the long term? The agreement was not perfect, and in light of the circumstances prevailing at the time, it could not have been. Foreign Minister Gruber had to take what Italian Prime Minister De Gasperi was prepared to give, and the latter also had certain interests to look after. Was the accord confirming in principle the Brenner border the right decision? The disappointment was particularly great among the Tyroleans, even though, as it turned out, it was a kind of Magna Carta for South Tyrol. In any case, over the following years, there was not a single Italian government that pursued a policy toward South Tyrol that could have been called "democratic." The majorification policy toward the *"allogeni"* was carried on, and some aspects of that effort would have made the Fascists proud, with the Italians themselves referring to it as their "51 percent policy."

There was not much sign of South Tyrol's "protector," Austria, during these years. The South Tyroleans were pretty much on their own, as Austria's attention was focused on the State Treaty that was signed in 1955. Austria now began to take a more active approach, one reason for which was the increasing pressure exerted by Tyrol on the federal government in Vienna. When talks with Italy brought no results, Foreign Minister Bruno Kreisky took this issue before the UN in 1960 despite massive pressure by the Western Allies not to do so. There, the Austrian delegation, with its tactic of calling for provincial autonomy for the "Austrian minority" in South Tyrol without the slightest mention of the Gruber-De Gasperi Agreement, found themselves without support. Had it not been for the British — Austria was Britain's partner in the European Free Trade Association — this could have turned into a disaster, which would not have displeased some Tyroleans at all and had even been their strategy. As one of them put it, "With this, we've burned our bridges behind us," and thus could even more justifiably demand self-determination, or perhaps even bomb it into existence under the (false) assumption of being able to unleash a partisan war in South Tyrol *à la* Cyprus or Algeria.

Italy maintained a consistent posture, insisting that the terms of the Treaty of Paris had been fulfilled, but was prepared to implement additional measures. Provincial autonomy was out of the question, however, to say nothing of self-determination. In the summer of

1961 the negotiations with Austria had broken down because Italy offered too little to satisfy the South Tyroleans, and the bombs began to go off in South Tyrol. Rome adroitly sought to initiate a dialogue with the South Tyroleans, who were hardly in a position to refuse. These talks did indeed come somewhere close to achieving a solution because of the new center-left government under Aldo Moro and Giuseppe Saragat, which had a new understanding for minorities. In 1964, one year after this government was formed, Kreisky thought that he and his Italian colleague Saragat had come up with a good solution. Before concluding what he called the "real secret negotiations" in Paris in December 1964, Kreisky brought North and South Tyrolean politicians together for a meeting in his home in Vienna where he got them to agree in principle to this solution "in order to avoid having it disavowed afterwards" as he said. But that is precisely what happened on 8 January 1965: the North and South Tyroleans said "no." Kreisky was outraged and disgusted and lost any desire to pursue the South Tyrol question any further.

In 1966, the conservative Austrian People's Party (ÖVP) solo government then wanted to bring the South Tyrol question to a quick conclusion — and initially failed to do so. The opponents of agreement could almost exult in their victory, and with them the terrorists, the persecution of whom by Austria had produced a number of errors and omissions. This went on until the summer of 1967 when Italy pulled the emergency brake and used its veto to block Austria's negotiations with the EEC. Austrian-Italian relations had thus reached their "lowest point since 1945."

Aside from determining the Package's contents, efforts during much of this period focused chiefly on "effectively anchoring it internationally." Austria and the South Tyroleans wanted to be assured that Italy would actually implement the measures that were promised in the Package, whereas Italy wanted to be assured that Austria would actually be ready to put an end to the dispute, following implementation of the Package. Italy refused to anchor the Package in a framework of laws. What finally emerged was the so-called operations calendar. The job at hand during the years that followed was the implementation of the Package, and that lasted all the way to 1992.

Looking back on the process of autonomy, in spite of all the problems and disappointments, one must say that the positive aspects rather outweigh the negative ones. The Treaty of Paris and the Package laid the groundwork for the survival of the German-speaking South Tyroleans in a foreign country. Despite having been separated from Austria for decades, the South Tyroleans speak their language just as before, live their lives, and carry on their customs and traditions. Bozen has indeed changed, but the villages of South Tyrol have remained Tyrolean villages. Over the last twenty or thirty years, there has been an incredible economic upsurge. There are no social tensions that cannot be overcome, and even political hostilities are often just spooks haunting the headlines of certain newspapers. Over the past ten to fifteen years, the province has had the lowest crime rate in Italy and virtually no unemployment.

Today, Italian culture and lifestyle are regarded by many South Tyroleans as an enrichment, a healthy portion of which would not do North Tyrol any harm either. For young people, mastering the Italian language has long been something taken completely for granted that opens up fresh new possibilities. The Brenner border was in fact an unjust boundary from the very beginning, but in recent years it has become increasingly permeable. In 1998, the barriers were removed at the crossings along that border, and there are not even inspections any more.

Bozen, March 1997: Luis Durnwalder (right) who succeeded Silvius Magnago as governor of South Tyrol in 1989, greets Italian President Oscar Luigi Scalfaro.

Even after 1945, however, Rome has not always made life easy for the South Tyroleans. Negotiations went on for two generations; the delays on the part of Italy made it difficult to speak sincerely of autonomy. There were many who absolutely refused to believe in it. But in 1992, autonomy was permanently established, and Austria and Italy declared their dispute to be ended. But that does not mean that all problems have been solved.

A minority — no matter how good its economic situation is at the moment — should never forget that it is a minority, and that it is impossible to regulate everyday life solely on the basis of codes of law. It always comes down to a minority's will to survive. When things are going well, survival perhaps becomes even more difficult and more complicated than during the hard times, even if that may seem at first glance to be a contradiction.

Things have been going well for the South Tyroleans in recent years; so well, that many have already forgotten the past. But a lack of knowledge about the past makes it hard to plan for the future. A somewhat more magnanimous attitude toward their fellow Italian citizens would surely do no harm today, even if the South Tyroleans never invited them there in the first place.

Notes

1. Eduard Reut-Nicolussi, *Tirol unterm Beil*, München 1928, p. 30.
2. Ibid., p. 84.
3. Enrico Baldini, *Storia e cronaca del 1922*, Merano 1988, p. 35.
4. Ibid., p. 40.
5. Reut-Nicolussi, *Tirol*, pp. 118-119.
6. Cf. Rolf Steininger, *Südtirol*, pp. 22-27, 77-80, 91 ff. (Steininger I)
7. Ibid., pp. 80–82.
8. Quoted by Maria Villgrater, "Katakombenschule," in: Klaus Eisterer/Rolf Steininger (eds.), *Die Option. Südtiol zwischen Faschismus und Nationalsozialismus*, Innsbruck 1989, p. 93.
9. Oswald Zoeggeler/Lamberto Ippolito, *Die Architektur für ein italienisches Bozen*, Lana 1992, p. 3.
10. Quoted in Leopold Steurer, *Südtirol zwischen Rom und Berlin 1919–1939*, Wien 1980, pp. 291-292.
11. Cf. Steininger I, p. 157.
12. Ibid., p. 160.
13. Karl Stuhlpfarrer, *Umsiedlung Südtirol 1939–1940*, Wien 1985, p. 24.
14. Cf. Steurer, *Südtirol*, pp. 443–445.
15. Ibid., p. 339.
16. Cf. Steininger I, p. 166.
17. Ibid., p. 168.
18. Cf. Steininger II, pp. 81–83.
19. Ibid.
20. Public Record Office [PRO, London], F[oreign] O[ffice] 371/50779/U 4311.

21. Ibid.

22. C.P. (Cabinet Paper) (45) 64, "Peace Treaty with Italy". Memo by the Secretary of State for Foreign Affairs, 5 July 1945. PRO, FO 371/50781/U 5519.

23. C.P. (45)64, "Peace Treaty with Italy." Ibid.

24. Top Secret, Charles to Under Secretary of State Oliver Harvey, 26 June 1945. PRO, FO 371/50780/U 5163.

25. 14 (45) Cabinet Conclusions, 12 July 1945. PRO, FO 371/50781/U 5518.

26. O.R.C. (45) 20, "Peace Treaty with Italy", memo by E. Bevin, 25 August 1945. PRO, FO 371/50782/ 6539.

27. Charles to Foreign Office, 28 August 1945. PRO, FO 371/50858.

28. PRO, FO 371/50929/U 4087. See also Foreign Relations of the United States [FRUS], 1945, vol. II, pp. 158-163, 170, 180.

29. "South Tyrol ought to be separated from Italy and reunited to North Tyrol and Austria. For this purpose a general voting by all inhabitants native to this country ought to be carried out ..." "What the South Tyroleans ask for." Memo by the Südtiroler Volkspartei, July 1945 sent to the Pope, the Allied Control Commission and all Foreign Missions in Rome. PRO, FO 371/50928.

30. Telegrams to Attlee, Truman, de Gaulle, Stalin, 28 August 1945. PRO, FO 371/46606/C 5460.

31. Parri to Truman, 22 August 1945; De Gasperi to Byrnes, 22 August 1945; Copies were given to the British. PRO, FO 371/50786/U 9339.

32. Meeting of the Cabinet, 5 September 1945; Conclusions No. 29. Records of the Chancellory, Vienna, Mack (Vienna) to War Office, 9 September 1945. PRO, FO 371/46606/C 5705.

33. Mack to Bevin, 13 September 1945; together with Austrian "Memorandum about the reincorporation of Southern Tyrol into Austria." PRO, FO 371/46606/C 6064.

34. Minute Cullis, 25 September 1945. Ibid.

35. Minute Burrows, 26 September 1945. Ibid.

36. Cf. e.g. Annex to secret U.K. memo "Austro-Italian Frontiers" for "Meeting of Foreign Secretaries in Paris," Brief No. 15, 19 April 1946. PRO, FO 371/55118.

37. Minute Cullis, 4 January 1946. PRO, FO 371/55117/C 39.

38. Memo Riddleberger, 3 January 1946. FRUS, 1946, vol. V, pp. 286-288.

39. Memo Reber, 7 January 1946. Ibid., pp. 288-289.

40. Handwritten minute Acheson, 9 January 1946. National Archives, Washington, Record Group 59, FW 863.0114-1-946.

41. Memo, 11 January 1946. FRUS, 1946, vol. V, p. 291.

42. Handwritten minute Reber, 13 January 1946. National Archives, Washington, Record Group 59, FW 863.01 14/1-1346.

43. Minute Cope, 10 January 1946. PRO, FO 371/50929/U 10358.

44. Minute Cope, 10 January 1946. Ibid.

45. Minute Cope, 10 January 1946. Ibid.

46. Minute Ross, 14 January 1946. Ibid.

47. Minute Hoyer-Millar, 19 January 1946. Ibid.

48. Minute Jebb, 4 March 1946. PRO, FO 371/57218/U 2759.

49. Minutes Cope and Ronald, 5 March 1946; ibid.; and UK Delegation, Paris, Brief No. 15, 19 April, 1946. PRO, FO 371/55118/C 5001.

50. Alan Bullock, *Ernst Bevin, Foreign Secretary 1945-1951*, London 1984, p. 242.

51. Ibid., p. 234.

52. Minute Ronald, 5 March 1946. PRO, FO 371/57218/U 2759.

53. Minute Jebb, 5 June 1946. PRO, FO 371/55121/CF 6336.

54. Cf. Martin Gilbert, *Winston S. Churchill*, vol. VIII, *Never Despair, 1945-1965*, Boston 1988, p. 260.

55. Sargent to Harvey, 11 July 1946. PRO, FO 371/55123/C 7631.

56. Sargent to Harvey, 3 August 1946; ibid.

57. Minute Sargent, 5 September 1946. PRO, FO 371/55124/C 9788.

58. Minute Dean, 22 August 1946. PRO, FO 55124/C 9728.

59. See Steininger III, p. 341.

60. Ibid., Doc. No. 58.

61. Ibid., Doc. No. 57.

62. Ibid., Doc. No. 59.

63. Confidential, Ashley Clarke, Rome, to Selwyn Lloyd, Foreign Office, 28 February 1959. PRO, FO 371/145031/RT 1081/8.

64. Record of conversation between the Secretary of State and Dr. Kreisky in Vienna, 25 June 1960. PRO, FO 371/153329/RT 1981/49.

The Gruber-De Gasperi Agreement

The Paris Agreement on South Tyrol

(The English text is original and definitive)

1. German-speaking inhabitants of the Bolzano Province and of the neighbouring bilingual townships of the Trento Province will be assured a complete equality of rights with the Italian-speaking inhabitants within the framework of special provisions to safeguard the ethnical character and the cultural and economic development of the German-speaking element.

   In accordance with legislation already enacted or awaiting enactment the said German-speaking citizens will be granted in particular:

   a) elementary and secondary teaching in the mother tongue;

   b) parification of the German and Italian languages in public offices and official documents, as well as in bilingual topographic naming;

   c) the right to re-establish German family names which were italianized in recent years;

   d) equality of rights as regards the entering upon public Offices with a view to reaching a more appropriate proportion of employment between the two ethnical groups.

2. The populations of the above-mentioned zones will be granted the exercise of autonomous legislative and executive regional power. The frame within which the said provisions of autonomy will apply, will be drafted in consultation also with local representative German-speaking elements.

3. The Italian Government, with the aim of establishing good neighbourhood relations between Austria and Italy, pledges itself, in consultation with the Austrian Government, and within one year from the signing of the present treaty:

a) to revise in a spirit of equity and broadmindedness the question of the options for citizenship resulting from the 1939 Hitler-Mussolini agreements;

b) to find an agreement for the mutual recognition of the validity of certain degrees and university diplomas;

c) to draw up a convention for the free passengers and goods transit between Northern and Eastern Tyrol both by rail, and to the greatest possible extent, by road;

d) to reach special agreements aimed at facilitating enlarged frontier traffic and local exchanges of certain quantities of characteristic products and goods between Austria and Italy.

(Signed)
Dr. Karl Gruber
Dr. Alcide Degasperi
5 September 1946

Chronology

26 April 1915	Secret treaty signed in London. The Entente Powers promise Italy South Tyrol — in return for Italy entering the war on their side against the Habsburg Empire and Germany.
10 Sept. 1919	Peace Treaty of Saint Germain. Tyrol is cut in two, South Tyrol is ceded to Italy.
24 April 1921	"Bloody Sunday" in Bozen.
October 1922	Mussolini takes over power in Italy: "Denationalization" of the German-speaking population; mass settlement of ethnic Italians in South Tyrol.
23 June 1939	Hitler-Mussolini Pact: The South Tyrolese are "forced" to choose between declaring themselves Italians or emigrating to Germany (the so-called Option).
5 Sept. 1946	Signing of the Paris Agreement by Italy's Prime Minister Alcide De Gasperi and Austria's Foreign Minister Karl Gruber. The Agreement envisaged special measures intended to preserve the ethnic identity of the South Tyrolese. It becomes an integral part of the Peace Treaty between the Allies and Italy.
31 Jan. 1948	First Statute of Autonomy. The provinces of Bozen and Trentino are merged into one region, which, as a consequence, has a majority of ethnic Italians. South Tyrol (Bozen) remains practically powerless. Important measures designed to protect the South Tyrolese are delayed.
17 Nov. 1957	Mass demonstration at Sigmundskron Castle near Bozen; 35,000 South Tyrolese, under the leadership of the new chairman of the South Tyrolean People's Party (SVP), Silvius

	Magnago, demand separation from the Trentino Province.
31 Oct. 1960	Austrian Foreign Minister Bruno Kreisky pleads the South Tyrol case before the General Assembly of the United Nations. UN Resolution 1497 urges Italy and Austria to find a solution for all differences relating to the implementation of the Paris Agreement.
11/12 June 1961	Wave of bomb attacks in South Tyrol.
5 Dec. 1963	Center-left government in Rome: Aldo Moro, Prime Minister; Giuseppe Saragat, Foreign Minister.
25 May 1964	Geneva Conference with the Foreign Ministers of Italy and Austria, Giuseppe Saragat and Bruno Kreisky; establishment of a joint committee of experts.
22 Nov. 1969	South Tyrol "Package" narrowly approved by SVP delegates.
29 Nov. 1969	Italian and Austrian Foreign Ministers agree on "Package" and "Calendar of Operation" about the implementation; subsequent approval by Italian and Austrian parliaments occurs.
20 Jan. 1972	Second Statute of Autonomy.
30 Jan. 1992	The last four steps of the "calendar" are implemented.
19 June 1992	The Austrian and Italian Permanent Representatives to the United Nations inform the Secretary General of the UN, Boutros Boutros-Ghali, that the dispute has ended.
2001	Extended autonomy for South Tyrol.

Abbreviations

ADERST	*Amtliche deutsche Ein- und Rückwanderungsstelle* (Official German Immigration and Remigration Bureau)
ADO	*Arbeitsgemeinschaft der Optanten* (Working Group for Those Opting for Germany)
AHB	*Andreas-Hofer-Bund* (Andreas Hofer Alliance)
APW	Armistice and Postwar Committee
BAS	*Befreiungsausschuss Südtirol* (South Tyrolean Liberation Committee)
CFM	Council of Foreign Ministers
CLN	*Comitato di Liberazione Nazionale*
CP	Cabinet Paper
CSCE	Conference on Security and Cooperation in Europe
EEC	European Economic Community
EUR	Office of European Affairs in the State Department, Washington, D.C.
FO	Foreign Office
FPÖ	*Freiheitliche Partei Österreichs* (Liberal Party of Austria)
GJR	*Gau-Jugend-Rat* (District Youth Council)
MP	Member of Parliament
MSI	*Movimento Sociale Italiano* (Italian Neofascists)
NA	National Archives, College Park, Maryland
NSDAP	*Nationalsozialistische Deutsche Arbeiterpartei* (National Socialist German Workers' Party)
ÖVP	*Österreichische Volkspartei* (Austrian People's Party)
PRO	Public Record Office, London
RM	*Reichsmark* (German Mark)
SOD	*Südtiroler Ordnungsdienst* (South Tyrolean Guard)
SPÖ	*Sozialistische Partei Österreichs* (Socialist Party of Austria)
SS	*Schutzstaffeln* (Protect Squads)
SVP	*Südtiroler Volkspartei* (South Tyrolean People's Party)
UN	United Nations

VKS   *Völkischer Kampfring Südtirols* (The People's Action Group of South Tyrol)

Further Literature

In English

Alcock, Antony E., *The History of the South Tyrol Question*, Geneva 1970.

Carandini, Niccolò, *The Alto Adige: An Experiment in the Devaluation of Frontiers*, Il Mondo 1958.

Fenz, Emanuel Gerson, *South Tyrol 1919 – 1939: A Study in Assimilation*, Ann Arbor, MI 1984.

Pfanzelter, Eva, "The South Tyrol and the Principle of Self-Determination: An Analysis of a Minority Problem," in: *Canadian Review of Studies in Nationalism*, Vol 1, 1998, p. 75–87.

Steininger, Rolf, "75 Years After: The South Tyrol Conflict Resolved," in: Günter Bischof/Anton Pelinka/Rolf Steininger (eds.), *Austria in the Nineteen Fifties. Contemporary Austrian Studies*, Vol. 3, New Brunswick – London 1995, pp. 189–206.

———, Back to Austria? The Problem of the South Tyrol in 1945/46, in *European Studies Journal* VII (1990), S. 51–83.

Toscano, Mario, *Alto Adige – South Tyrol: Italy's Frontier with the German World*, Baltimore 1975.

In German

Alcock, Antony E., *Geschichte der Südtirolfrage: Südtirol seit dem Paket*, Wien 1982.

Eisterer, Klaus/Steininger, Rolf (Hrsg.), *Die Option: Südtirol zwischen Faschismus und Nationalsozialismus* (Innsbrucker Forschungen zur Zeitgeschichte 5), Innsbruck 1989.

Gatterer, Claus, *Im Kampf gegen Rom: Bürger, Minderheiten und Autonomien in Italien*, Wien, 1968.

Gehler, Michael (Hrsg.), *Verspielte Selbstbestimmung? Die Südtirolfrage 1945/46 in U.S.- Geheimdienstberichten und österreichischen Akten: Eine Dokumentation*, Innsbruck 1996.

Lill, Rudolf, *Südtirol in der Zeit des Nationalismus*, Konstanz 2002.

Messner, Reinhold (Hrsg.), *Die Option. 1939 stimmten 86 Prozent für das Aufgeben ihrer Heimat. Warum? Ein Lehrstück in Zeitgeschichte*, München 1989.

Solderer, Gottfried (Hrsg.), *Das 20. Jahrhundert in Südtirol*, Bozen 2000.

Steininger, Rolf, *Los von Rom? Die Südtirolfrage 1945/46 und das Gruber-De Gasperi-Abkommen* (Innsbrucker Forschungen zur Zeitgeschichte 2), Innsbruck 1987.

——, *Südtirol im 20. Jahrhundert. Vom Leben und Überleben einer Minderheit*, Innsbruck, 1997, 1999³.

——, *Südtirol im 20. Jahrhundert. Dokumente*, Innsbruck, 1999.

——, *Südtirol zwischen Diplomatie und Terror 1947–1969, Darstellung in drei Baenden: Bd. 1: 1947–1959, Bd. 2: 1960–1962, Bd. 3: 1962–1969*, Bozen 1999.

——, *Südtirol 1918–1999*, Innsbruck, 1999.

——, *Alto Adige/Sudtirolo 1918–1999*, Innsbruck, 1999.

Steurer, Leopold, *Südtirol zwischen Rom und Berlin 1919–1939*, Wien 1980.

Acknowledgements

The publication of this book has been made possible through the friendship treaty between the Universities of New Orleans and Innsbruck and the generosity of these two institutions. The Dean of Metropolitan College and Vice Chancellor of Strategic Planning and Budget Robert L. Dupont and Professor Franz Mathis, the Senate-appointed coordinator of New Orleans affairs for the University of Innsbruck, have supported this project in every possible way. Vice-Rector Professor Peter Loidl of the University of Innsbruck and Dr. Mathias Schennach from the *Auslandsamt* of the University of Innsbruck have provided vital financial support, so has the Provincial Government of South Tyrol, and Dr. Benita Ferrero-Waldner, the Austrian Minister for Foreign Affairs. *Ministerialrat* Alois Söhn and Gottfried Prinz from the Austrian Ministry of Education, Culture, and Science have provided funds for the translation of this volume. Mel Greenwald and Dr. Margaret Davidson translated parts of it from German into English. Dr. James Davidson, professor emeritus in political science from Tulane University, gave the text a close read from the perspective of an interested American audience.

We owe Jennifer Shimek from Loyola University New Orleans an extraordinary debt of gratitude for her competent copy-editing and professional typesetting of the manuscript. Eva Plankensteiner and Ingrid Voggenberger at the Institute of Contemporary History at the University of Innsbruck and Gertraud Griessner at the University of New Orleans' CenterAustria have made this work much easier in the transmission and handling of the manuscript, photos, and facsimiles between Innsbruck and New Orleans.

As always, it has been a pleasure to work with the professionals at Transaction — Irving Louis Horowitz, the founder, publisher and chairman, who gave this text an extraordinary warm welcome; Mary Curtis, the President; and Anne Schneider, our remarkably cooperative editor. Ellen F. Kane put her usual artistic skills towards the production of a wonderful cover.

Günter Bischof, New Orleans
Rolf Steininger, Innsbruck

Index

A

Acerbo, Giacomo, 18
Acheson, Dean, 85, 152
ADERST, 64
ADO, 64, 67
Adriano Colocci-Vespucci, 51
Agricultural Central Bank, 34
AHB, 74
Alfredo Giarratana, 26
Alleanza Nazionale, 75
Allied Council, 82
Allies, 68, 75, 80, 82, 118, 145, 146
Alpenzeitung, 26, 71
Alpini Monument, 38
Amonn, Erich, 75, 76, 110, 114
Amplatz, Luis, 127, 128
Amtliche deutsche Ein- und Rückwandererstelle, 64
Andreas Hofer Association, 9
Andreas-Hofer-Bund, 74
Andreotti, Giulio, 140, 142
Arbeitsgemeinschaft der Optanten, 64
Archivio per l'Alto Adige, 15, 40
Athesia, 3, 21, 71
Attlee, Clement, 82, 92, 151
Attolico, Bernardo, 50, 52
Auschwitz, 72, 73
Austrian Civil Law Code, 34
Autonomy Statute of 1948, 21, 110, 116, 133, 135
Autonomy Statute of 1972, 21

B

Bacher, Gerd, 123
Badoglio, Pietro, 36
Barbesino, Luigi, 6
Barello, Mario, 39
BAS, 123, 125
Battisti, Carlo, 75
Battisti, Cesare, 36, 37, 38
Beer Hall *Putsch*, 52
Befreiungsausschuss Südtirol, 123
Behrends, Hermann, 55
Bene, Otto, 53, 57, 61, 68
Benedikter, Alfons, 132
Berlin Agreement, 56
Berlin Wall, 139
Bevin, Ernest, 79, 82, 89, 91, 92, 95, 97, 151, 152
Bischoff, Norbert, 106
Bloody Sunday, 1, 6, 9
Bocchini, Arturo, 53, 58
Bonomi, Ivanoe, 10
Bormann, Martin, 55
Bottai, Bruno, 142
Boutros-Ghali, Boutros, 144
Bozen Museum, 40, 42
Bozner Nachrichten, 25
Bozner Tagblatt, 71
Brenner Pass, 1, 4, 48, 80, 81, 83, 84
Brugger, Peter, 132
Buffarini-Guidi, Guido, 58
Bulgaria, 5
Burggraefler, 25
Burrows, B.A.B., 82, 151

Byrnes, James, 80, 151

C

Cadorna, Luigi, 36
Carandini, Niccolò, 103, 106, 108, 109
Catholic Action, 46
Catholic Church, 1, 62, 63
Catholic Youth League, 47
Cavallaro, Pietro, 36
CFM, see Council of Foreign Ministers
Charles, Nöel, 79, 86, 151
Churchill, Winston, 98, 152
Ciano, 52, 53
Ciano, Galeazzo, 52
Clarke, Ashley, 118
CLN, 74
Club Alpino Italiano, 23
Cold War, 2, 1, 77, 92, 145
Comando Supremo, 5
Comitato di Liberazione Nazionale, 74
Commission for the Language and Culture of the Oberetsch, 42
Commission of Nineteen, 125
Commission of Nine, 136
Commission of Six, 136
Commission of Twelve, 136
Commissions of Six and Twelve, 141
Communism, 85, 86, 88, 92
Conference on Security and Cooperation in Europe, (CSCE), 143, 144
Constitutional Law Nr. 1, 134
Cope, Charles, 86, 87, 152
Corbino, Mario, 9

Council of Deputies, 95
Council of Europe, 118, 131
Council of Foreign Ministers, (CFM), 79, 80, 82, 85, 86, 87, 89, 92, 95, 97
Credaro, Luigi, 8
Crupi, Attilio, 9
CSCE, see Conference on Security and Cooperation in Europe
Cullis, Michael F., 82, 151

D

Dachau, 61, 68, 73, 76
Dalsass, Joachim, 132
D'Annunzio, Gabriele, 37
Dante Alighieri Society, 14, 16
Day of the Army, 38
Dean, Patrick, 98, 101
de Michelis, Gianni, 140
De Gasperi, Alcide, 80
de Murville, Couve, 95
de Stéfani, Alberto, 12
de Steffanini, Antonio, 34
Decree Nr. 2525, 34
Decree Nr. 7622, 33
Delueg, Simon, 11
Der Landsmann, 21, 25
Der Tiroler, 19, 21
Die Abendpresse, 123
Die Presse, 123
Dietno, Walter, 30
District Youth Council, 46
Dolomiten, 25, 26, 71, 76, 112
Draft Peace Treaty, 77, 78, 79
Drusus, 37, 41
Duce, see *Il Duce*
Durnwalder, Luis, 140
Dwarf King Laurin, 41

E

Eden, Anthony, 78, 79
EEC, see European Economic Community
European Economic Community, (EEC), 128, 129, 130, 131, 133, 147
Egarter, Hans, 74
Eisenhower, President Dwight D., 119
Elisabethschule, 12
Ellmenreich, 26
Endrici, Celestino, 37, 60
Ente di Rinascita Agraria per le Tre Venezie, 33
Entente Powers, 5
ERA, 33, 35
EUR, 85
European Free Trade Association, 146
Express, 123

F

Facta, Luigi, 10, 12
Falck Group, 44
Fanfani, Amintore, 39, 128, 130
Fasci di Combattimento, 6
Fascio, 6, 8
Fedele, Pietro, 36
Feltrinelli-Masonite Corporation, 43
FF, 138
Figl, Leopold, 82, 83, 97, 104, 118
First Autonomy Statute in 1948, 35
Fort Otto Huber, 123
FPÖ, see *Freiheitliche Partei Österreichs*
France, 48, 67, 91
Freiheitliche Partei Österreichs, (FPÖ), 133
Führer, 46, 48, 49, 55, 58, 62, 67, 91
Führer principle, 46

G

Gamper, Michael, 25, 29, 74, 112
Gatterer, Claus, 32
Gau-Jugend-Rat, (GJR), 46
Geisler, Johannes, 62, 63, 73
Gentile, Giovanni, 18, 26
German National Socialist Workers' Party, 47; see also *Nationalsozialistische Deutsche Arbeiterpartei*, NSDAP
German Teachers College, 26
Gestapo, 72
Giolitti, Giovanni, 9
Giornaletto, 15
Giunto, Francesco, 12
Giurati, Giovanni, 37
Göring, Hermann, 52
Gouin, Félix, 82
Greece, 51, 91
Greil, Wilhelm, 23
Gruber, Karl, 2, 3, 80, 82, 94, 95, 97, 101, 102, 103, 105, 106, 107, 108, 109, 110, 118, 137, 142, 145, 146
Gruber-De Gasperi Agreement, 101, 137, 142, 145, 146
Gschnitzer, Franz, 117
Guadagnini, Giuseppe, 21, 31
Guerriero, Augusto, 12
Gypsies, 59

H

Harvey, Oliver, 88, 89, 151, 152
Heinburg, Kurt, 52

Heinricher, Kurt, 46
Helm, Robert, 46
Hillebrand, Rolf, 46
Himmler, Heinrich, 50, 52, 54, 55, 58, 59, 67, 68
Hitler, Adolf, 46, 91
Hofer, Andreas, 9, 62, 69, 70, 71, 73, 74, 80, 92, 94
Hofer, Franz, 2, 67, 68, 69, 71
Hofer, Peter, 47, 48, 58, 61, 62, 64
Hood, Samuel, 87
Hoyer-Millar, Frederick, 88, 152
Hungary, 4, 5

I

Il Duce, 32, 35, 39, 48, 124; see also Mussolini, Benito
Il Trentino, 71
Innerhofer, Franz, 8
Innerkofler, Adolf, 23
Innocenti, Silvio, 105, 110
Innsbrucker Nachrichten, 22
International Court, 143
Istituto De Agostini, 18
Istituto di Storia per l'Alto Adige, 20
Italian Neofascists, 75; see also Movimento Sociale Italiano, MSI

J

Jebb, Gladwyn, 89, 91, 94, 95, 152
Jews, 59, 72

K

Kappler, Herbert, 70
Kardaun Power Plant, 44
Kennedy, John F., 119, 120

Kerbler, Christian, 128
Kerschbaumer, Sepp, 123, 127
Klaus, Josef, 133, 150, 165
Klotz, Georg, 127, 128
Kompatscher, Andrae, 41
Kögel, Fritz, 15
Kreisky, Bruno, 117, 119, 121, 128, 130, 146, 147, 153
Kronen, 5

L

La Nazione Italiana, 14
La Provincia di Bolzano, 26
Ladins, 10, 15, 135
Lancia Group, 44
Lancia Works, 44
Lateran Treaties, 28
Laurin Fountain, 40, 41
Law, Richard, 33, 34, 77, 103, 134
Lex Corbino, 9
Lex Gentile, 26, 27, 29
Lill, Rudolf, 35
Lira, 21, 54, 71
Lire, 21, 24, 36, 39, 54, 114, 115
Lloyd, Selwyn, 118
Lorenz, Max, 52, 53
Lucifero, Roberto, 118
Luig, Wilhelm, 64

M

Mack, William, 94, 96, 97, 151
Magistrati, Massimo, 52
Magnago, Silvius, 114, 116, 125, 130, 132, 139, 140, 142
majorification, 20, 33, 145, 146
Manci, Gianantonio, 70
March on Rome, 10, 12

Mastromattei, Giuseppe, 45, 53, 57, 60
Matthews, Freeman H., 86
Mauthausen, 73
Mayr, Michael, 51
Mayr-Falkenberg, Ludwig, 68
Measures for the Industrial Development of the Community of Bozen, 43
Menz-Popp, Josef, 76
Meraner Zeitung, 25, 26
Minerva, 15
Ministerial Armistice and Postwar Committee, 77
Misuraca, Giuseppe, 63
Mitterdorfer, Karl, 132
Mock, Alois, 143
Moggio, Vittorio, 9
Molden, Fritz, 123
Molotov, Wjatscheslav, 95
Montecatini Corporation, 43
Montecatini Works, 124
Moro, Aldo, 129, 130, 132, 147
Moscow Declaration, 77
Movimento Sociale Italiano, 75; see also Italian Neofascists, MSI
MSI, 75, 113
Mumelter, Norbert, 46, 49
Mussolini, Benito, 1, 9, 11, 12, 21, 22, 26, 28, 33, 35, 36, 37, 38, 39, 43, 44, 48, 49, 52, 53, 57, 58, 65, 66, 68, 69, 75, 92, 98; see also *Il Duce*

N

National Assembly, 5
National Association of Alpine Soldiers, 39

National Socialism, 1, 46, 47, 58, 74, 76
Nationalsozialistische Deutsche Arbeiterpartei, 47; see also German National Socialist Workers' Party, NSDAP
NATO, 119
Nazis, 46, 48, 50, 55, 59, 60, 71, 84, 85
Nenni, Pietro, 131
Nibelungen, 29, 56, 57
Nicolussi, Karl, 62
Night of Fire, 122, 124
North Atlantic Treaty Organization, (NATO), 119
NSDAP, 47, 71; see also German National Socialist Workers' Party, *Nationalsozialistische Deutsche Arbeiterpartei*

O

Oberhammer, Aloys, 123
Office of European Affairs in the State Department, 86
Official German Immigration and Remigration Bureau, 64
One Tyrol, 139
ÖVP, see *Österreichische Volkspartei*, People's Party
Optanten, 67, 105
Option, 1, 20, 46, 49, 50, 51, 54, 55, 58, 60, 62, 63, 64, 116, 150, 165
Österreichische Volkspartei, (ÖVP), 130; see also, People's Party

P

Package, 2, 112, 129, 130, 131, 132,

133, 135, 136, 137, 138, 139, 140, 141, 142, 144, 147, 148
Paris Agreement, 101, 110, 116, 117, 121
Paris Peace Conference, 18
Parri, Ferruccio, 80, 151
Patentino, 137
Peace Conference, 82
Pecori-Giraldi, Guglielmo, 4
Pella, Giuseppe, 113
People's Action Group of South Tyrol, 30, 46
People's League, 51
People's Party, 2, 39, 75, 80, 130, 147; see also *Österreichische Volkspartei*, (ÖVP)
Perassi, Tommaso, 110
Perathoner, Julius, 12, 40
Pétit Parisien, 33
Pfaundler, Wolfgang, 123
Piacentini, Marcello, 36
Piccolo Posto, 13
Pius XI, 28
Place Name Decree, 25
Podestà, 24, 41, 42, 71, 113
Police Law of 1925, 33
Pompanin, Alois, 62
Popolo d'Italia, 13, 33
Postal, Giovanni, 127
Press Law, 25
Preziosi, Giovanni, 18, 52
Proporz, 137
Proporz Decree, 137
Provincia di Bolzano, 71
Prunas, Renato, 103, 106, 108

R

Raab, Julius, 117, 119

Raffeiner, Josef, 76
Raffl, Johannes, 28
Raiffeisenkasse, 34
Rava, Pietro, 41
Reber, Charles, 85, 86, 152
Reichenau, 72
Reichsmark, 54
Renner, Karl, 6, 81, 82, 94
Renzetti, Giuseppe, 52
Resolution 1497/XV, 121
Reut-Nicolussi, Eduard, 5, 150, 165
Ricci, Umberto, 33
Riddleberger, James, 85, 86, 151
Riz, Roland, 132, 140, 141, 142
Rohmeder, Wilhelm, 51
Ross, Archibald, 88, 152
Rossi, Paolo, 129
Rumor, Mariano, 133
Russia, 88, 91, 95

S

Sacred Heart of Jesus Festival, 124
Sargent, Orme, 89, 98, 152
Scelba, Mario, 125
Schmid, Heinrich, 106
Schoefl, Hans, 102
School Law, 26
Scotti, Vincenzo, 144
Scuola Regina Elena, 12
Second World War, 1
Seipel, Ignaz, 37
Sforza, Carlo, 84
Sigmundskron, 73, 115, 116, 123
Simonetti, Gustavo, 127
Socialist Party, 130
Società Italiana per il Magnesio, 44
SOD, 70, 72
South Tyrolean Farmers'

Association, 34
South Tyrolean Guard, 70
South Tyrolean Liberation Committee, 123
South Tyrolean Savings Bank, 34
Soviet Union, 87, 89, 97
Soviets, 80, 91
Sozialistische Partei Österreichs, (SPÖ), 130, 133
SPÖ, see *Sozialistische Partei Österreichs*
SS-*Polizei*, 70
Stafflmayr, Emil, 143
Stalin, Josef, 82, 151
Starace, Achille, 6
State Treaty, 2, 117, 146
Steurer, Leopold, 54, 55, 56, 150, 165
Stresemann, Gustav, 40
Stuhlpfarrer, Karl, 52, 150, 165
Südtiroler Heimatfront, 47
Südtiroler Ordnungsdienst; see SOD
Südtiroler Volkspartei, (SVP), 2, 29, 75, 76, 80, 82, 109, 110, 112, 114, 116, 117, 123, 125, 127, 129, 130, 132, 136, 137, 138, 139, 140, 141, 143
SVP, see *Südtiroler Volkspartei*
Syndicate of Farmers, 34

T

Tambroni, Fernando, 119
Taviani, Paolo Emilio, 39
Tinzl, Karl, 33, 67, 74
Tiroler Anzeiger, 22
Tirolia, 21
Tolomei, Ettore, 1, 13, 14, 15, 16, 17, 18, 19, 20, 21, 35, 36, 40, 41, 42, 51, 52, 60, 68, 75, 124
Ton•i•-Sorinj, Lujo, 128, 130
Treaty of Paris, 101, 117, 133, 142, 143, 144, 146, 148
Treaty of Saint Germain, 6
Troutbeck, John, 88
Truman, Harry S., 80, 82, 151
Turkey, 5, 51, 91
Tyrol Castle, 11
Tyrolean Farm Rule, 34

U

United Nations, 2, 81, 104, 117

V

Vatican, 28, 60, 63
Venezia Tridentina, 8, 10, 11
Viberti Auto Body Plant, 44
Vichy government, 67
Victor Emanuel III, 18, 36
Victory Monument, 1, 35, 37, 38, 39
Vittoria Sagittaria, 37
VKS, see *Völkischer Kampfring Südtirols*
Völkischer Kampfring Südtirols, (VKS), 1, 30, 46, 48, 49, 55, 56, 57, 58, 59, 61, 64, 66
Vogelweider, 21, 25
Volgger, Friedl, 60, 61, 74, 76, 102, 114, 132
Volksblatt, 25
Volksbote, 25, 26, 29
von Bern, Dietrich, 41
von der Vogelweide, Walther, 2, 19, 40
von Engert, Baron, 81
von Guggenberg, Otto, 102, 108, 110

von Hassell, Ulrich, 52
von Ribbentrop, Joachim, 52
von Sternbach, Lothar, 57
von Sternbach, Paul, 33
von Weizsaecker, Ernst, 52
Vranitzky, Franz, 143

W
Waffen-SS, 69
Waldheim, Kurt, 131, 133
Walther Monument, 40, 41
Walther Square, 2, 19

Wehrmacht, 58, 70, 75
Western Powers, 81
Wimmer, Lothar, 106
Wochenpresse, 123
Wolff, Karl, 58, 66, 69
Working Group for Those Opting for Germany, 64
World War I, 16, 35, 39, 48, 57, 59, 84

Y
Yugoslavia, 91, 92

Lightning Source UK Ltd.
Milton Keynes UK
UKOW03f0333050614

232851UK00001B/19/P